PARTNERING WITH PARENTS IN YOUTH MINISTRY

JIM BURNS AND MIKE DEVRIES

Gospel Light

Gospel Light is a Christian publisher dedicated to serving the local church. We believe God's vision for Gospel Light is to provide church leaders with biblical, user-friendly materials that will help them evangelize, disciple and minister to children, youth and families.

It is our prayer that this Gospel Light resource will help you discover biblical truth for your own life and help you minister to youth. May God richly bless you.

For a free catalog of resources from Gospel Light, please contact your Christian supplier or contact us at 1-800-4-GOSPEL *or* www.gospellight.com.

PUBLISHING STAFF
William T. Greig, Chairman
Kyle Duncan, Publisher
Dr. Elmer L. Towns, Senior Consulting Publisher
Pam Weston, Managing Editor
Patti Pennington Virtue, Associate Editor
Jessie Minassian, Editorial Assistant
Bayard Taylor, M.Div., Senior Editor, Biblical and Theological Issues
Robert Williams, Cover Designer and Cover Production
Debi Thayer, Designer

ISBN 0-8307-3229-2
© 2003 Gospel Light
All rights reserved.
Printed in the U.S.A.

HOW TO MAKE CLEAN COPIES FROM THIS BOOK

You may make copies of portions of this book with a clean conscience if
- you (or someone in your organization) are the original purchaser;
- you are using the copies you make for a noncommercial purpose (such as teaching or promoting your ministry) within your church or organization;
- you follow the instructions provided in this book.

However, it is illegal for you to make copies if
- you are using the material to promote, advertise or sell a product or service other than for your ministry fund-raising;
- you are using the material in or on a product for sale; or
- you or your organization are not the original purchaser of this book.

By following these guidelines you help us keep our products affordable.

Thank you,
Gospel Light

DEDICATION

To the thousands of youth workers who are trying to figure out how to reach kids more effectively and partner with their parents. You are some of the finest people in the universe. Your dedication and commitment to being world changers is nothing short of miraculous.

Jim Burns and Mike DeVries

CONTENTS

ACKNOWLEDGMENTS

This book is truly the result of many incredible thinkers and outstanding youth workers. First and foremost, we are grateful to our families who put up with this passion of ours and sacrificed our time and attention while we wrote this book.

In 2002, several key youth-ministry specialists contributed to our thinking and to a national seminar YouthBuilders put on around the country. A most special thanks to Mark DeVries and Doug Berny. Although our names are on this book, without your help, insight, stories, friendship, inspiration and role modeling, there would be no book. You are the best.

Thank-you to the YouthBuilders staff. You are amazingly dedicated and continually giving of yourselves. We are honored to call you partners in ministry and blessed to call you friends.

Thank-you to the hundreds of YouthBuilders trainers and associates who have shared some of this material with people around the world.

A special thank-you to Judy Hedgren for your patience and great help in making the manuscript for this book presentable.

We are also grateful to our friend Pam Weston and her team at Gospel Light. Thanks for your belief in this project and your patience and grace with our late submission. We owe you!

Jim and Mike

INTRODUCTION

As youth workers, we know that renewal and revival most often come when a younger generation has the courage to pray life-changing prayers and take a radical stand for Jesus Christ. Many in today's generation of young people are doing just that. What an honor to see firsthand God's incredible movement in the world of youth ministry. I count it one of the great privileges of my life to serve alongside so many wonderful committed women and men in the youth-ministry movement around the world.

I believe we are in the midst of a "transitional generation" in the history of youth ministry. As with all movements of God, it is easier to define what a generation experiences in hindsight than it is to define the experience as it occurs. I am the least qualified to name what this new, fresh wind in youth ministry will be called, but I do believe that it will have something to do with recognizing family-based youth ministry as part of a healthy transformation in our mission. The history of youth ministry is just over 150 years old, yet many of us are only now recognizing how critical the family is to a young person's spiritual formation and discipleship.

This book is a humble approach to rethinking church youth ministry. We are not suggesting a radical change in programming. What we are suggesting is a fresh mind-set: Parents and family are crucial to faith development in every area of a ministry's program.

We are grateful you have picked up this book and look forward to a continual dialogue and learning experience with you. As you daily jump into the trenches and make a huge difference in the lives of kids and their families, do not hesitate to call on us if there is anything we can do to come alongside you.

Thank you for making an eternal difference.

Jim Burns, Ph.D.
President, YouthBuilders

SECTION 1

THE STRATEGY

CHAPTER ONE

FAMILY-BASED YOUTH MINISTRY—A MIND-SET, NOT A PROGRAM

When you welcome a child you welcome me.
(SEE MARK 9:37.)

If you reach the family, you reach the world.
BILL BRIGHT

The role of the Church is to mentor parents, the role of the parent is to mentor their children, and the legacy of faith continues to the next generation.
ED COLE

Those three quotes to the side of my (Jim's) desk encourage me to do what I do every day. Josh McDowell recently told me that in 1945, more than 70 percent of the population in Great Britain attended church each Sunday—today, that figure is only 7 percent. What happened?

Church historians tell us that the Church in Great Britain, as well as most of Western Europe, missed just one generation of young people and their families; the result was almost a deathblow to the Church.

Culture watchers, including George Barna and Josh McDowell, report that more than 80 percent of the students attending church while in high school will *not* attend church one year after they graduate.

Judges 2:10 tells us:

> After that whole generation had been gathered to their fathers, another generation grew up, who knew neither the LORD nor what he had done for Israel.

What can the Church today do to make sure this is not our story? We are very confident that this does not have to be the direction the Church goes, and we believe God is raising up a new biblical approach to strengthening His church in this generation. This approach is called family-based youth ministry, and it is a strategy for taking seriously the biblical mandate for the Church to partner with parents and build into the spiritual life of kids *together*.

A short time ago, as I walked outside of my house early one morning to pick up the newspaper, I observed a young man running down my street away from an older man with a knife in his hands. I froze and watched what seemed like a slow-motion movie right in front of my house. I was jolted back into reality when the older man screamed to me, "Call the police, he has been robbing our neighborhood!"

Although I had never (thank God) had the need to call the police in an emergency before, my adrenaline took over. I rushed inside, dialed my telephone and excitedly began to describe in great detail to the woman who answered just exactly what was taking place. I found myself telling her the best location to park the police cars and how to find the young man. Once I took a breath, the woman calmly asked, "Sir, what would you like me to do about it?" Shocked at her response, I said, "Pardon me?" She replied, "Sir, you have reached 4-1-1, the number for information." Aghast, I quickly hung up and called the right number, but I was too late—the thief got away.

Why did you need to hear that story? Here's the deal: *I had the right motives but the wrong number.* Is it possible that the Church and the modern-day youth-ministry movement has had the right motives for reaching out to young people and their families but has been dialing the wrong number? I think so.

FAMILY—THE MOST POWERFUL INFLUENCE

Long after students stop attending youth groups, they are still connected to their families. Although there are wonderful adult conversions and a growing movement of reaching students from non-Christian homes, by far the most influential people in a young person's spiritual life are his or her parents. Of course, this gives us great hope mixed with a bit of pessimism, because anyone who has been in youth ministry for more than 30 minutes knows that historically there has been a disconnection between parents and teens when it comes to spirituality. This is precisely why we believe it is time for the Church to come back to its roots of doing a more effective job of partnering with parents.

In this new generation of youth ministry, the Church will need to focus more on serving the family as a whole. George Barna's research is showing that somewhere around 85 percent of people who make a commitment to Jesus Christ are making that commitment before the age of 18—those who don't make the commitment by this age probably *never* will.[1] Several years ago I conducted a poll with key youth workers around America and Canada, and I asked, "What are you doing to help families succeed?" Across the board, their answers were almost identical: "I know that working with families and parents is very important—and it's my top goal for *next* year." Most of the youth workers I know are still trying to get a grasp of this important but elusive part of ministry. They know that families are important to the spiritual growth and well-being of their students, but they don't know how to fit ministering to these families into their already overcommitted schedules.

Some youth ministry experts would say that the recent advance of family-based youth ministry has been a refreshing wind blowing in the Church. Others would say they are still looking for a simple definition or a program to help make sense of how to do family-based youth ministry in a practical way. I (Jim) can still remember reading my good friend Mark DeVries's book *Family-Based Youth Ministry* the very week it was published in 1994. (In fact, I've read and enjoyed most of the books written on this subject!) This book was—and is—one of the most important new paradigms for youth ministry in decades. That said, I am still looking for a practical handle, or description, for how to *do* family-based youth ministry.

Ray Whitson is a veteran youth worker, YouthBuilders associate and all-around-great youth-ministry leader in Illinois. He is partnering with parents and doing family-based youth ministry in a huge way and probably doesn't even know it. I recently ran into Ray at the National Youth Workers Convention. When I asked him how he was doing, he shared that he had been through a rough season of ministry. A few weeks before the convention, Ray received a horrible phone call—one of his students had committed suicide. Immediately, Ray went to the distraught family. He sat with the parents, threw a football out in the yard with the young man's two teenaged brothers and helped clean up the young man's room. Finally, back home that same night, he was exhausted and feeling the strain of the day. As he lay in bed and shared the pain of the day with his wife, the phone rang. It was the same family Ray had just spent time with. This time, Ray was told that the father, an elder in Ray's church, had been robbed and shot four times and was in critical condition at the hospital. Once again, Ray stood by this family, and Ray and his wife even took care of the two teenaged boys while their mother nursed their father back to health—all while the family was still grieving over the loss of their son and brother.

This type of situation is not a normal daily occurrence for most of us, thank God. However, most days in youth ministry we are trying to help families succeed whether we realize it or not. Perhaps we have not always been able to get a handle on family-based youth ministry because we are more involved in it than we realize. That is definitely Ray's story. You see, partnering with parents is a mind-set, not a program.

Although I'm still looking for an easy definition, a defining moment came for me at the Western (Wailing) Wall in Jerusalem. I stood with my family and a few friends watching several bar mitzvah celebrations taking place. The young Jewish teens were surrounded by family members cheering them on as they read and quoted from memory words from the Torah. It was an incredibly moving experience to watch the fathers and mothers, aunts and uncles, grandparents, siblings and friends all take an active role in each young man's spiritual life. It reminded me of a very special experience for my family when our Jewish neighbors invited us to the worship service and celebration for their daughter's bat mitzvah. The family involvement in this coming-of-age for a young Jewish boy or girl is incredible.

To be honest, I found myself a bit jealous that the Jewish faith has such an incredible ceremony and we Christians do so little with this special rite of passage. Then I remembered way back to my seminary days and an obscure lesson I had long since forgotten. My professor told us about the Shema, found in Deuteronomy 6:4-9, which is the most often quoted Scripture in the entire Bible. He told us that every morning and every evening of every day the Orthodox Jews recite this important section of the Torah. This Scripture is written on the door frames of Orthodox Jewish homes. It is the essence of the Old Testament summed up in a few sentences. In fact, the Shema was no doubt one of the first Scriptures Jesus would have learned as a child. When He was asked, "What is the greatest commandment?" (see Mark 12:28), the young Jesus surely quoted the Shema:

> Hear, O Israel: The LORD our God, the LORD is one. Love the LORD your God with all your heart and with all your soul and with all your strength. These commandments that I give you today are to be upon your hearts. Impress them on your children. Talk about them when you sit at home and when you walk along the road, when you lie down and when you get up. Tie them as symbols on your hands and bind them on your foreheads. Write them on the doorframes of your houses and on your gates.

To this day, there is not a practicing Jew alive who cannot quote from memory these verses. Is it possible that they are more important to future effective youth ministry than we dare to imagine?

When I considered the Shema after my time at the Western Wall, what I saw was very different from what I had expected. In biblical days the people of Israel had a much better understanding of their role as parents and family. They knew it was their most important calling to impress upon their children the Word of God. They were to talk about it and live out their faith daily as a family unit. Each child knew his or her place in the family and in the faith. This Scripture is the very cornerstone of family-based youth ministry! Part of the responsibility of a youth worker is to reach students by strengthening families to *impress* the Word of God into their hearts and minds. For the first time I looked at a ministry to parents not as one more program or on the peripheral but as central to my calling in youth ministry. I will dare to say it again: Family-based youth ministry is a mind-set, not a program!

The job of the Church is to keep the priority of family at the fore-front of our mission, to give families the understanding and tools they need to raise their children to continue to grow their legacy of faith. There are no easy answers here, just solid truths: We are all called to do family-based youth ministry, we must help families succeed, and we must change our mind-set and make the biblical principle to equip families to succeed a part of daily youth ministry.

THE POWER OF THE FAMILY IN SPIRITUAL FORMATION

In order to change our mind-set, we need to embrace the realization of the power of the family in spiritual formation. Consider the following statistics:

- A 1993 study commissioned by *Newsweek* magazine and the Children's Defense Fund revealed that the following factors were most influential on kids (in order): parents, extended family, coaches, teachers and other adults outside the home, peers and media.[2]
- According to Abilene Christian University, students who reported having positive family communication were twice as likely to perceive God as important in their lives than those who reported negative family communication.[3]
- A 1993 study by the Search Institute revealed that nothing influences the faith maturity of teenagers as much as "family religiousness."[4]
- According to a 1997 study conducted by Barna Research, 78 percent of youth indicated that their parents had more influence on their decision making than anyone else in their lives.[5]

Here is the bottom line: Students are influenced more by their parents than any other single group—including their peers—and those who lack adult (especially parental) influence are more likely to give in to peer pressure.

If we truly desire to be more effective in seeing the lives of our students transformed into the likeness of Christ, the greatest resource we have is the greatest influence in their lives—their parents. Our goal is to come alongside parents to help them pass on the faith to their children. We also take students who come from families that do not profess Christ and assimilate them into the Church body as extended family (more about this in chapter 6). Family-based youth ministry is about changing how we view the work of youth ministry. We should never underestimate the power of parents in the spiritual formation of their children. If spiritual formation is the key—and we believe it is—parents are too valuable to leave out of the equation. We need to bring parents into the circumstances and situations of their children, affirming and helping to reestablish parental roles in the spiritual formation of our students.

Before we make any decisions to spend more time partnering with parents or changing our programs, we need to make sure we understand the incredible evolution of the family over the past generations. In chapter 3 we invite you to take a peek at the ever-changing family system and how it affects our ministry to students.

Notes

1. George Barna, "Teens and Adults Have Little Chance of Accepting Christ as Their Savior," *The Barna Report* (October-December 1999), n.p.
2. Wayne Rice and David Veerman, *Understanding Your Teenager* (Nashville, TN: Word Publishing, 1999), p. 118.
3. "Real Faith in a Virtual World" (pamphlet presented at the Fifteenth Annual Conference on Youth and Family, Abilene Christian University, Abilene, TX, 1999), p. 5.
4. Peter L. Benson and Carolyn H. Elkin, *Effective Christian Education: A National Study of Protestant Congregations: A Summary Report on Faith, Loyalty and Congregational Life* (Minneapolis, MN: Search Institute, 1990), p. 62.
5. George Barna, "Teenagers (age 13 to 18)," *Barna Research Online*. http://www.barna.org/cgi-bin/PageCategory.asp#ParentsofChildren (accessed June 5, 2003).

THE PILLARS
OF PARTNERING
WITH
PARENTS

There are no clear-cut, off-the-shelf, by-the-book models for a family-based approach to ministry. You will not find a just-add-water or one-size-fits-all program guaranteed to transform your ministry instantaneously into what it should look like. There is no one right way to be family based—no cookie-cutter mold we need to fill. There are going to be some familial similarities, but just as our students and their families are diverse, so will the expression of that similarity take on many forms.

You may have heard of the six-to-one ratio: six students for every one leader. Have you ever thought about what might happen if we were to change that ratio to mean six leaders for every one student? What might happen if every student in your youth ministry had a network of people reaching, encouraging, supporting, praying for and building up him or her? How might that change the youth-ministry setting? The results would be staggering.

In order to have a lasting influence in the lives of our students, we must involve and connect with their parents. This is the difference between throwing students a rope and building a net! Consider the experience of the men who helped build the Golden Gate Bridge in San Francisco, California:

Some newspapers called it the "Dance of Danger." It was a technique of constructing bridges while on top of swaying catwalks and high towers. Sometimes hundreds of feet in the air, the scaffolding would be regularly tossed and blown by the wind. This dance yielded a calculated fatality rate—for every one million dollars spent, one life would be lost.

Engineers of the Golden Gate Bridge believed that the risks could be lowered. When construction began in 1932, numerous safety measures were put in place. At the end of construction the cost towered at 20 million dollars, yet only one worker died. How did they do it?

For the first time in bridge construction, a highly effective safety device that had been proven useful by circus trapeze acts was put into place. A net was hung below the high-flying scaffolding, draping 60 feet below the roadbed under the construction and extending 10 feet to either side. Although costing $130,000, this new measure was so effective that local newspapers began running box scores with headlines like, "Score on the Gate Bridge Safety Net to Date: Eight Lives Saved!" Those who had fallen and been saved by the net were said to have joined the Halfway-to-Hell Club.[1]

Many students today are on a spiritual high wire. More often than not the Church has attempted to reach out to students by throwing them a rope and hoping they would grab hold. For many of us in youth ministry, the scenario is more like trying to throw a rope to five falling kids at once! Family-based youth ministry takes a different approach: investing in the construction of a safety net to place underneath students—one that will both reach out to and support them. An important element of the net is parents, but it may also include volunteers, small-group leaders or even elderly men and women in the church who will pray daily for a handful of students.

As mentioned earlier, there will be some similar characteristics between family-based approaches. But they are just characteristics. How you express them in your ministry will be shaped by your passion, vision and specific situation. Each youth-ministry setting is unique. That said, there are four common pillars in every successful family-based ministry.

PILLAR ONE: COMMUNICATE

How can the youth ministry in your church be more effective for you? I (Jim) and many youth workers I know have posed this question to parents over and over again through the years. The overwhelming response is that parents want *information*. They want communication about events, topics being covered in the youth group and other general information. We cannot assume that students are keeping their parents informed about what's going on. We must make it a point to help parents feel like they are a part of the team in ministering to their children.

FOUR KEY CONCEPTS

In youth ministry, communication with parents can sometimes be haphazard at best. Yet clear communication is the first hallmark of a quality, family-based youth ministry. When people have the right information, they feel connected to the ministry and will be much more apt to support the direction and vision of that ministry. There are four key concepts that will help you communicate clearly with the parents of your students.

One—Keep Parents Updated

Parents need accurate, available and advance information concerning your youth ministry and youth group events. They need to know that they have quick access to the most important information, whether it is through a web page specifically designed for this purpose or a 24-hour telephone information line they can call.

Two—Share Your Vision

Parents need to know your heart and your vision. The greatest downfall for many youth workers is not lack of vision but inability to communicate and pass along their vision to others. It doesn't matter that you have a phenomenal plan if you can't get others to catch the vision. (For more information on clearly and concisely communicating a strategy to others, we recommend *Purpose-Driven Youth Ministry* by Doug Fields.[2])

Three—Display Your Passion

Parents need to know your passion. For any effective partnership to take place, both parties need to hear and understand one another. Parents need to know where you've come from and to hear and understand your heart and your passion for their children and the ministry their children are involved in. They need to know that you are there to support them and not to compete with them. In this way your hearts will be united in purpose and vision.

Four—Provide an Open Forum

Parents need avenues through which to dialogue about the needs and issues they are facing with their children. Most parents of teens feel desperately alone in dealing with the struggles of parenting. Some feel inadequate and struggle with a deep-seated loneliness in that area. During the course of any group setting in which you have brought parents together in a room, you are bound to hear one parent ask another, "You deal with that too?" and "Wow, I thought I was the only who couldn't figure it out." Parents need to know they are not alone; they need to feel a sense of community and connection with you and with other parents. They need a place to talk, a place to be honest and a place to share their children's needs with the ministry leaders.

So what does partnering with parents look like? Let's say you're planning a camp or retreat for your students. Weeks before the event, you schedule an evening of sharing the vision and the direction of the camp with parents. But wait! How have you gone about informing parents about this meeting? Did you rely on your students to relay the invitation to their parents? Not! If you have thought this through (and of course you have), you or someone on your leadership team has personally contacted the parents of each of your students, shared the purpose of the meeting and invited the parents to attend. In addition, parents have been asked questions such as "Is there anything we need to know about your child before we leave for this event?" and "Are there any specific concerns that we can help you address with your child?"

At the informational meeting, you share the camp speaker's topics and pray together with parents for the ministry during the event. You ask for a parent who doesn't mind being called by the other parents to act as the communication hub for the group during the event, and you make sure each family has this person's phone number. This person will be the one you call during the time away at the event, and other parents will call to get reports from that parent. Finally you offer supplemental devotional materials for the family to use when the students come home.

While on the trip, use a cell phone to keep the contact parent updated. (Be sure to call often!) Share the joys and the needs that have presented themselves. Maybe there is something parents can be praying about. Utilize the contact parent to relay important information from other parents to you or to their children. During the trip home, update the contact person on your progress and your arrival status. (This concept can also be done with a voice mailbox.)

After the retreat, have a debriefing with parents. Share the experience with them. You might want to have photos and/or video from the retreat available. Have a few of the small-group leaders share about their ministry for the week or weekend. Share the joys of what's going on with students. All parents love to hear others affirming their children!

Here are several more ways to develop good communication with parents:

- **Parent Information Night**—At least twice a year, sponsor an informational meeting to present the parents with all the information they need—and some information they don't know they need. Have some of your "point" parents help you plan the agenda; they'll have a good idea of how well other parents know what's going on and what parents are concerned about. We have found that young youth workers (without teens of their own) don't always understand what the parents' felt needs are. Be sure to honor the parents with good communication, good food, good fun—and don't let the meeting drag on. Make it *the* meeting to attend at your church so that they'll want to come back.
- **Parent Newsletter**—A great way to keep communication lines in place is through a simple but well put together parent newsletter. Find someone in the church (student or parent) who will handle the graphic design and layout. Fill the newsletter with information about upcoming events,

Bible study topics and perhaps a short parenting article from an expert or a cartoon about the family. Keep it newsy and easy to read. Some churches are moving from a paper newsletter to a Web-based letter. If you choose to go that route, be sure to print out and keep a supply of the newsletter for new families in the church and for families who do not have Internet access.

- **24-Hour Information Line**—How about developing your own youth-group phone line just for information? It can be for parents and for students. Each week have someone cleverly update the information on times, schedules, upcoming events and anything else that seems important. On the weekend of a youth retreat, call in updates on the phone line.

- **Dedicated Website**—You can offer much of your information on a good youth-group website. You probably have a student or parent who could use their talents to design the site and act as Webmaster. The website can be a great tool for information and also a platform to provide resources, such as family-friendly links (like YouthBuilders.com), special articles, Bible studies and so much more.

- **Community Awareness**—One of the simplest (but very much appreciated) pieces of information you can provide parents with is information on community events and/or experiences that will help sharpen their parenting skills. If the local hospital or community college is sponsoring a seminar or special class, let the parents know about it. If a speaker or event is coming to your town, keep the parents informed with a special community calendar of events.

PILLAR TWO: ENCOURAGE AND EQUIP

I (Jim) never understood how difficult it is to parent teens until I had three teenaged daughters of my own! I now know that I need all the encouragement I can get! If one thing is certain, it is that being a parent is *tough*. Partnering with parents is about building bridges and connections with one another. Nothing does that better, or more effectively, than a ministry of affirmation and equipping. Parents who feel connected, affirmed and equipped by the youth leaders will support and believe in the direction of the ministry.

ENCOURAGING PARENTS

Just as we need to have a ministry of affirmation in the lives of students, affirmation needs to be characteristic of our ministry with parents. The terrain parents must travel is riddled with battles and trials, counterbalanced by periods of growth and intimacy with their teenagers. Youth workers have to assume that parents are not having an easy go at raising their teens. This is an open opportunity to partner with parents. They need to know that their parenting efforts truly matter and that they are making a difference in their child's life. Every time you give a parent the gift of encouragement, you are doing family-based youth ministry.

A phone call, a note, an e-mail of encouragement, a meal shared together, simply sitting with the parents at their son or daughter's events—whatever the venue—it is important to create opportunities to affirm parents both in words and actions.

EQUIPPING PARENTS

A family-based youth ministry must equip and empower parents to engage their children in spiritual development. It is not enough for us just to encourage or affirm parents. As we've already mentioned, Deuteronomy 6:4-9 places parents at the heart of spiritual influence in the lives of their children. The role of the Church should be one of supporting parents as they take on the primary role of the spiritual development of their family.

Imagine that a student in your ministry is depressed over her grades. As the youth leader, you spend an hour encouraging this student in her studies, and she begins to feel better about herself as she makes a commitment to work toward bringing her grades up. When she goes home, everything you have talked about suddenly goes right out the window because her parents start criticizing her for what they perceive as her academic laziness. Ouch! How can you avoid this scenario? One way is to take five minutes to make a phone call to the parents and say, "Here's what I'm doing. How can I support what you're doing?"

The equipping part of family-based ministry is a mixed bag—as a youth worker you may be wondering if *you* are equipped enough to equip parents! Never fear; this is where the word "assistance" applies. Perhaps you can't make a presentation to parents on teen depression, but you can assist them by arranging a seminar and inviting an expert to speak on the subject of teen depression. You can also encourage, equip and assist parents by simply posting the names and phone numbers of qualified Christian counselors (whom you have personally interviewed) on the bulletin board or wall in your office.

Here are several more ideas for encouraging and equipping parents:

- **Have an annual "Celebrate Parents Day."** At least once each year, dedicate a day to honor the parents at your church. I thought it was a lousy idea until I became a parent—now I'll take any encouragement I can get. Make the day affirming and meaningful.
- **Do the little things.** Just as you would for a student, write a note of encouragement or make a brief phone call to parents simply to compliment them on something their child did or something the parent did for their child.
- **Change the scenery.** Contact work is a major part of youth ministry; supporting and encouraging students in their activities outside your youth group is important. Turn this support and encouragement into a family affair by taking the opportunity to sit with the parents sometimes. Some of my best conversations with parents have been at their kids' school events.
- **Identify and affirm inherited character traits.** Here's one idea that will bless the socks off parents! Think of a positive character trait (or two) that a parent possesses and that you see reflected in the life of his or her child. For example, compliment a parent by saying, "Thanks so much for your help with the student trip. I've noticed that Lisa has developed such a servant's heart, and I can see where she gets it."

PILLAR THREE: INVOLVE

While it is true that not all parents should be youth leaders, there is a lot more potential for involving parents than many of us realize. Kids need parent and grandparent role models just as much as they need young adults.

What if a student doesn't want his or her parent to be involved in the youth group? Most kids would probably be OK with their parent being a youth leader, but others might feel like their parents are stealing some of their personal youth-group time. Dialogue and compromise need to prevail. One of my (Jim's) daughters is a great kid and is active in our church and in the Fellowship of Christian Athletes (FCA). She doesn't mind if Mom or Dad speaks once in a while or if the group meets at our home—but during this season in her life, she would rather not have us as her main youth leaders. We need to abide by her wishes. Of course, she is the one who said, "Dad, all of my friends think you are so cool. You are like the favorite dad." When I asked her if *she* thought I was cool too, she quickly responded, "No!" So for now my wife and I are back to making sure there's plenty of good food at our house.

Some parents would be wonderful as leaders and mentors. This is especially important in a world where many students have parents who don't attend church.

Here are a few ideas for involving parents in your ministry:

- **Adult Sponsor Team**—Our experience has been that a diversity of staff is the best way to provide role models for kids. Many of the larger youth groups shy away from adult sponsors because they "just aren't cool enough." This is a major mistake because while some may not be cool, they are a healthy necessity for a well-rounded staff. Part of healthy youth ministry is providing examples of Christ-centered marriages and people who bring their Christian faith into their parenting practices. Parents even teach from a different level of experience than others. (Some parents, of course, are better suited for serving the ministry in the prayer fellowship, advisory council, socials or retreats areas.)
- **Prayer Fellowship**—Hold a weekly prayer group for both

parents and students. This can be one of the more powerful parts of your ministry. (Note: It is important to make sure the time is truly a powerful time of prayer and not a gossip session.)

- **Parent Advisory Council**—Parents who are not particularly gifted at working directly with kids may have gifts in counsel and support. A parent advisory council is akin to a youth-group booster club whose purpose is to provide wisdom, support and counsel. Some parent advisory councils meet quarterly, and many have raised thousands of dollars for youth mission or camp experiences.
- **Socials**—Socials are an opportunity to bring parents and their kids together for pure fun. These gatherings can range from more formal banquets to outrageously messy theme nights, sporting events, game nights—you name it. Anything goes as long as it's a family-bonding time sponsored by the church.
- **Retreats**—If you have ever facilitated or even attended a retreat, you'll no doubt agree that two things are sure to happen to the majority of people who attend a retreat: (1) they will make an important spiritual decision (whether accepting Christ for the first time or making a commitment to follow Him more closely), and (2) they will connect with others. What could be more powerful than a yearly parent/teen getaway with all the elements of fun, spiritual challenge, interaction and togetherness that characterize a retreat? Rebecca and I (Jim) are still experiencing the positive effects of a retreat we attended together this past year.

PILLAR FOUR: REACH OUT

Healthy family-based youth ministries can be powerfully evangelistic. Even non-Christian parents have a deep love and concern for their children and have a heartfelt desire to be good parents. Since family-based youth ministry is about supporting and encouraging parents in their role, we as youth workers are placed in an influential position also to share the love of Christ with these parents. What better way is there for us to introduce parents to the life-changing power of Christ than by entering into their families as a support and example?

When non-Christian parents see a youth leader's love and concern for their children, they sense that they are not the only ones who want the best for their children, and this opens doors for ministry to the entire family—and changing lives for eternity. Our vision must include reaching out to the non-Christian parents of our students. Partnering with parents in all stages of spiritual maturity is an investment in the spiritual legacy of the entire family.

Here are some helpful suggestions for reaching out to parents:

- **Sponsor special seminars for parents**. Wanting the best for their kids can be a powerful draw for non-Christian parents to attend seminars designed to help them improve or expand their parenting and family skills. (See chapter 10 for a list of our favorite seminar titles.)
- **Offer family-counseling opportunities**. When families are in trouble, they often look for counseling and advice. Non-Christian parents seeking help for their problems will welcome any help they can get. If your church offers counseling, great; if not, make sure to have counseling referral information readily available.
- **Incorporate big brother and big sister programs**. Some churches have started big brother and big sister programs for kids from single-parent families. Many single parents look for a church with a program like this, in which church members "adopt" one or two kids to include in their family activities. These couples also schedule one-on-one time with the "adopted" kids. This type of program not only gives kids the opportunity to interact with two-parent families but also demonstrates support and care for the single parents by giving them a break.
- **Offer divorce recovery workshops**. It's a fact: The majority of today's families do not look like the television shows of the 1960s (for that matter, neither did the families then!). Divorce-recovery workshops are an excellent way to minister

to Christians and to reach hurting non-Christians with the healing that only Jesus can provide.

If you wonder about whether or not reaching out to parents can make a difference in their lives, consider the following true story about how a ministry in which Jim was involved helped change one woman's life:

Molly Brewer (not her real name) is a grateful parent. As a newly single mom still reeling from a devastating divorce, Molly turned to the local church for help with her kids. Although she had accepted Christ as a child, Molly strayed from her faith in college and, as a sign of her independence during this rebellious period, had married an unfaithful man. After her husband admitted to years of infidelity, the marriage blew apart. Because she was completely broken and because of her concern for her two children, she looked for and found a loving church home.

Molly's kids immediately connected with the youth group, but Molly was reticent to become involved, sharing with a friend that she felt "different" than most of the families she saw arriving at church each Sunday. But the more her kids became involved in their youth group, the more Molly was drawn to the church.

One day Molly received an invitation to attend a parents information night hosted by the youth-group leaders. It was at this meeting that Molly met other single moms and was invited to join their weekly Bible study. Later, she attended a divorce-recovery program, and the church helped her with some family counseling.

Before Molly knew it, the church was her place of refuge—her lifeline. Today she is on the parent advisory committee for the youth group and her faith is vibrant and growing. Molly recognizes that what began with a family-friendly youth group and a loving church helped spiritually energize her and her children, and although there are still consequences to go through because of her past decisions, Molly knows that she is on a new road thanks to a simple but life-changing ministry that dared to care for a *family*.

Notes
1. For more information, visit http://www.goldengatebridge.org/research/Construction BldgGGB.html.
2. Doug Fields, *Purpose-Driven Youth Ministry* (Grand Rapids, MI: Zondervan Publishing House, 1998).

THE EVOLUTION OF THE FAMILY

In order to partner with parents effectively, youth workers must become students of the culture. Incredible changes have taken place in the family over the past few decades, and we must have an understanding of both the way families were in the past and the reasons for how they are today. Perhaps we need only look as far as our TV sets and take a stroll down memory lane with TV families. There are people who say that art imitates life; others say that life imitates art. We think that perhaps it's a little of both. The truth is that TV families have changed over the past half century in a way that mirrored—and quite possibly influenced—family life in the real world.

THE PAST 50 YEARS—A RETROSPECTIVE

THE 1950S

The Adventures of Ozzie and Harriet TV show captured the sense of family in the 1950s—a time period in which 93 percent of households with children had both parents present.[1] This fictional family was played by the real-life Nelson family. Fumbling dad, Ozzie, offered semicoherent advice; wise and efficient mom, Harriet, held the family together like a general; and children David and Ricky were well groomed and well behaved. Life, according to the fictional Nelsons, was simple, and all problems could be solved in a matter of 26 minutes (only four minutes of commercials—ah, the good old days).

THE 1960S

The simplicity of the 1950s gave way to the turbulent 1960s. The nuclear family was still the prevailing family model but changes were brewing. In the 1960s, the percentage of households with children in which both parents lived was down to 90.9.[2] The Vietnam War, race issues, social revolutions and the emergence of the "generation gap" began to put a strain on the nuclear family. On TV, *The Munsters* and *The Flintstones* replaced the Nelson family, and the nuclear family began to be viewed as an unrealistic dream. Three shows with single dads arrived on the scene: *Bonanza*, *The Courtship of Eddie's Father* and *My Three Sons*. (Ironically, *The Munsters* had a more realistic family model, as single dads headed up only about 3 percent of families.)[3]

THE 1970S

The 1960s practically explode into the 1970s. Disco; punk, permed and Farrah Fawcett hairstyles; platform heels; casual sex and drug use—the 1970s were absorbed by a sense of unrestrained freedom. Economics began to force moms into the workplace, and the Watergate scandal breathed an air of cynicism into the fabric of American culture. Of all the changes, one outweighed them all: a newfound freedom with divorce. Nearly 25 percent of all marriages ended in divorce in the 1970s.[4] As the family continued to deteriorate at an alarming rate, only 88.6 percent of households in this decade had both parents living under the same roof.[5] *The Brady Bunch* emerged as the new family model; yet a more accurate portrayal of reality was found in *All in the Family's* social-debating, ever-widening generation gap, free discussion of casual sex, open bigotry and an unemployed parent. *One Day at a Time*, a sitcom about a divorced mom, reflected the real-life situation of almost 5.5 million families.[6]

THE 1980S

The 1980s marked the return of conservatism, both in politics and pop culture. Commonly referred to as the decade of material prosperity, this decade also saw a marked trend in one-parent households. By the 1980s, only 80.4 percent of households still had both parents living under the same roof.[7] The generation gap of the 1960s was officially over, and TV shows like *Family Ties* portrayed the kids as being more conservative than their aging hippie parents. *The Cosby Show* was the first TV series starring an affluent black family, and its hallmark was the loving and often humorous relationship between husband and wife, Cliff and Clair Huxtable. The "all togetherness" of *The Cosby Show* was offset by the rise of another TV phenomenon, *Roseanne*, which offered just the opposite of the Huxtable household. Where *The Cosby Show* offered sound advice and stability, *Roseanne* offered chaos and irony. Dan and Roseanne Conner as parents were caricatures and any normalcy offered came from the children. Economic turmoil and tough-love parenting, mixed with an exuberant dose of sarcasm, were the defining characteristics of the Conner family.

THE 1990S

Cultural diversity, economic explosion and an alarming divorce rate were the cornerstones of American society in the 1990s. In the early part of the decade, the divorce rate climbed to nearly 50 percent of all marriages and then leveled off as the new millennium approached. Only 75.9 percent of all households could boast a mom and dad living at the same address.[8] The TV-family revolution started by *Roseanne* continued with the highly dysfunctional *The Simpsons* cartoon, which became the standard characterizing American family life, using satire and sarcasm to delve into the social issues of the '90s—everything from toxic waste to violence, from homosexuality to human cloning. Quintessential Gen-Xer Bart Simpson's badge of honor was underachievement, yet his views on family and social issues clearly reflected the stance of the culture: Everything is suspect, everything is seen through a lens of cynicism, what works is right, and what's moral is relative.

TODAY

The new millennium was rushed in with an increased push by kids to enter adulthood. Children today are growing up too soon by being forced to see and deal with reality (an exaggerated reality) prematurely. The Internet rules the day and economic uncertainty abounds. The World Trade Center attacks changed everyone; life is different now. Yet the family trends of the past half-decade continue. Now only 72.9 percent of all households in America have two parents still married to each other.[9] The TV family has turned from fantasy to "reality" with *The Osbournes*. British rocker Ozzy Osbourne, known in past decades as the self-proclaimed Prince of Darkness, is now seen as a harmless, inept father and husband who seems constantly to be either running around the house yelling at his kids, "I don't care what you think, I'm the [bleep]ing Prince of Darkness!" or needing the assistance of his wife, "Sharon!" The show's dialogue (which seems to feature more bleeps per half hour than all of TV history combined) focuses on a family on the verge of meltdown and its family issues of open drug use, arguments over curfew, having boyfriends and girlfriends spend the night, piercing and tattooing. All the while—and *frighteningly*—it's the drug- and alcohol-abusing kids who appear to display the most maturity!

The question remains: Does art imitate life or does life imitate art? Only the next decade will reveal the truth.

THE GENERATIONAL CYCLE—WE WERE THEIR AGE, BUT WE WERE NEVER THEIR *AGE*

Families are different today because individuals within the families have changed; however, most of what our students are going through is very similar to what their parents (and their parents before them) went through. Why do we say this? Because regardless of their generation, all human beings want to be accepted, to find their place in this world and to have a personal identity. The difference is that each subsequent generation deals with these identity issues in a radically different social context, in the matrix of their own unique adolescent culture. To understand each other fully, we need to have a broader understanding of the cultures in which we made those crucial decisions.

Generational studies have much to tell us about family-based youth ministry. Each generation has its strengths and weaknesses, and while individuals within a generation may vary, their peer pool shapes their perceptions and worldviews. Individuals born near the beginning or end of a generation may also have some of the defining characteristics of the neighboring generation.

In their book *Generations: The History of America's Future, 1584 to 2069*, researchers Neil Howe and William Strauss identify four major generation types that continually cycle (with isolated exceptions): Civic, Adaptive, Idealist and Reactive.[10]

(GI) Civic	(Silent) Adaptive	(Boomers) Idealist	(Gen X) Reactive	(Millennial) Civic
Born 1901-1924	Born 1925-1942	Born 1943-1960	Born 1961-1981	Born 1982-2003
Characterized by principles of God, country, patriotism Motto: "Do the right thing because it is the right thing to do."	Adapted principles from previous generation Motto: "It worked for them; it will work for me."	Independent, materialistic and driven; look out for number one Motto: "I will do what is best for me."	Reactive, less enthused and less hopeful about future; felt impact of previous generational values Motto: "What's the use?"	The new Civic—Postmodern and Millennial Motto: "Tell me the truth and show me where I belong."
Community ➡		*Individualism* ➡		*Community*

GENERATIONS DEFINED
Here is a brief definition of the four major generation types:

1. **The Civic Generation**—Commonly called the GI generation for their contribution in World War II, this generation was shaped by a spiritual awakening born out of years of depression and great need. The GI generation owned the values they trusted because they had come by them the hard way. The identity of the GI generation was forged out of fiery trials, and

they came to embrace a way of life that was marked by loyalty and honor. (Important Note: We'll elaborate more on Millennials, the new Civic generation, later in this chapter.)

2. **The Adaptive Generation**—This generation is sometimes called the Silent generation, because they imitated what the generation before them demonstrated. They held many of the same values but had less ownership of them. This generation benefited from the sacrifices made by the previous generation and began to embrace a time of prosperity and hope for the future. Longing to fulfill their dreams and empower the next generation, their loyalty to community was present, but they occasionally felt they had to look out for their own.

3. **The Idealist Generation**—Also called the Boomer generation, this group came equipped with the resources and personal drive to reach greater heights of accomplishment and financial success than any previous generation. They rode into this time of prosperity on the sacrifices of the previous generation, and they were convinced that nothing was out of their grasp. Idealistic and independent, loyalty was merely a means to climb the next rung of the corporate ladder. Looking out for number one and independence were treasured values. But independence has its price. While this generation will be remembered as one of the most economically successful and accomplished generations, they will also be remembered as one of the loneliest.

4. **The Reactive Generation**—Also known as Gen X, this was a generation of latchkey kids. Many were raised in single-parent homes and immersed themselves in gadgets and techno-gizmos. Disenchanted with what they had, they longed for something more yet weren't sure what they were looking for or what they needed. Paying the price for the independence movement begun by the Boomers, Gen-Xers weren't sure whom to trust and were characterized by less confidence in the future.

As much as those born to a generation would like to think that their generation is the best one, the truth is that each generation needs the other. Understanding another generation means exploring the events and attitudes that have shaped their view of the world because their worldview determines why they feel, value and react in the manner they do. As we seek to understand other generations, we learn to appreciate the forces that shape those people—and us.

Family-based youth ministry is about being a student of the generations, not merely the current culture. As we understand the influences that shape generations, we are better equipped to help adults help kids. Family-based youth ministry is as much a means of ministering to parents and grandparents as it is ministering to students. Our role is to facilitate the narrowing of generational misunderstandings.

UNDERSTANDING YOUR STUDENTS—SOME DEFINING CHARACTERISTICS OF THE NEW CIVIC GENERATION

It's difficult to place Millennials into a nice, neat box with a clear label (which oddly enough is a characteristic of this generation itself). The members of the new Civic generation

- Care more about community and less about individualism
- Are tired of interpretations; want to know what is true and trusted
- Have a desperate desire to experience truth through the stories of others; are less impressed with a list of dos and don'ts and propositional truth
- Need to be connected to family or community
- Measure personal value by how they are loved
- Want to do something significant—not so they leave their mark on the world, but so the world's mark on them is not so deep, dark or painful
- Are a wellspring of compassion waiting to be tapped; have experienced personal pain or the pain of their peers, making them more genuine conduits of grace and mercy to others
- Are bombarded with moral relativism; constantly exposed to hearing "That's great that it is true for you, but I see it another way."

- Have a deep spiritual hunger and a desire to connect with something bigger than themselves—something transcendent (experiential and participatory worship and liturgy is returning with this generation)
- Desire authenticity and genuineness; skeptical of excellence for its own sake
- Are moved by honesty and transparency; the more real Christianity is presented, the more apt they are to investigate the truth claimed
- Balance the dichotomy of being hopeful and skeptical at the same time—hopeful of what the future might hold (including their contribution to it), but battle with the same skepticism of the previous generation (status quo is stale; change is fresh)
- Recognize that they are inundated with perhaps more choices than any previous generation; often backlash against the consumerism of pop culture and the media

While great programs may have been the approach for earlier generations, making students feel they belong is the key to reaching this generation. The more that authenticity and genuineness characterize our ministry, the better. Effective ministry will be marked by the ability to create a sacred space in which our students encounter God and build community, not by how great our games are.

Effective family-based youth ministry is about bringing the generations together in mutual respect and understanding. This will be accomplished through empowering and equipping parents to influence the spiritual development of their children and instilling in children a heartfelt respect for their parents. Think about the importance of family-based ministry this way: Very few people are in therapy because of dysfunctional friends, but many are in therapy because of dysfunctional families!

Notes

1. Andre Mouchard, "From Ozzie to Ozzy: America's Demographics Have Changed, but TV Families Still Sell Love and Stability—in Many Forms" *Orange County Register*, April 23, 2002, n.p.
2. Ibid.
3. Ibid.
4. Ibid.
5. Ibid.
6. Ibid.
7. Ibid.
8. Ibid.
9. Ibid.
10. William Strauss and Neil Howe, *Generations: The History of America's Future, 1584 to 2069* (New York: Morrow, 1991). Used by permission.

BUILDING A STRATEGY FOR FAMILY-BASED YOUTH MINISTRY

Doug Berny is one of our family-based youth ministry heroes. He was the youth pastor at Max Lucado's church in San Antonio, Texas, and he took a gutsy stand when he introduced the family-based ministry concept to his new congregation in Nashville, Tennessee.

One of the key leaders in his new church asked Doug to spend some time in a discipleship relationship with the leader's son. He shared with Doug that his son was going through a very important time in his life and that there were some important topics to cover. The dad also mentioned that he was busy with his business responsibilities and just couldn't find the time to talk with his son about important subjects like sex and sexuality, faith and other issues. Doug, a true discipler, liked the young man, but there was just one problem: If Doug discipled the son, it meant the father was forfeiting his God-ordained role to disciple his son through this important rite-of-passage season in his life. (Note: This does not mean that there is not appropriate discipleship that can and should take place between youth workers and students.)

Doug told the leader that he would think about what he was asking of Doug and get back to him. The leader made it clear that this was really what the church had hired Doug to do, so he shouldn't take too much time thinking about it.

After a great deal of thought, Doug approached the father and told him that he would *not* disciple his son but that he would agree to meet regularly with the man to help him learn to disciple his own son. The father was not pleased, but Doug stuck to his guns, even after the father complained to the pastor. (Fortunately Doug had already used much of the commonsense strategy explained later in this chapter, and the pastor supported Doug's decision.) Today there is a young man in Nashville who has been blessed by a discipleship relationship with his once-reluctant father. The father, by the way, now says that discipling his son has been one of the finest experiences of his life.

A veteran youth worker and friend of ours came to one of the family-based youth ministry conferences sponsored by YouthBuilders. When I (Jim) asked him if he was doing much in the area of partnering with parents, his response was actually quite enlightening: "Oh, when the idea first came out, I tried to implement it, but it didn't work, so I'm back to basically ignoring the parents." Oops! He didn't get it. Developing the mind-set of partnering with parents to enhance the spiritual growth of *their* kids is central to all aspects of youth ministry. Let us say right now that your actual youth programming and events may not change much. Few family-based youth-ministry models that have dramatically changed their programming have worked well. Think of this strategy as *enhancing* your existing youth-ministry program, not completely renovating it. The following definition, slipped into my hand after a conference, says it all:

Family-based youth ministry is a paradigm, not a program. It is ministering to youth in the most biblical and effective way possible by equipping and empowering the most influential people in a teenager's life—their parents.

You will still have camps, mission experiences, Bible studies, outreach events, prayer times and all the other things you normally have; however, you will now do each program with the overarching knowledge that your students are deeply connected with and affected by their family system. (For example, my family background involved some alcoholism, and I'm just now learning how that issue has affected my spiritual life and my relationships.)

This chapter will outline the basics of how to establish and present the idea of a more family-friendly youth ministry. You'll have to decide which ideas will and won't work for your particular situation, but the basic, intuitive strategy can actually be applied to any type of new emphasis you may be presenting to your church. We call this the commonsense approach to introducing a strategy. Once you have developed a strategy, get ready to put on your sales-and-marketing hat to help your congregation get it.

PRESENTING A COMMONSENSE STRATEGY

Have you ever read a book or come home from a conference fueled with new ideas, programs and strategies—all of which you want to try out in the next week?

Remembering that partnering with parents is much more a mindset than a program will help you avoid the burnout that comes from trying to do too much at one time. It's always a good idea to start change slowly. Change small things first in order to see victories, but always have a bigger vision in mind. Start slow—change only one or two things at first—then move on to other changes only after the old changes have become a natural part of what you are doing. Keep this goal in mind: bringing young people to a more mature faith in Jesus Christ by helping them build a foundational love relationship with God that reaches into every area of their life. Giving your youth ministry a family-friendly focus is not an overnight process, but it can—and will—bring about dynamic change. The key is thinking in advance thoughts such as, *What red flags will I possibly encounter? What issues stand in the way of changing our ministry mind-set?* and *How will I address them?*

FIVE STRATEGY STEPS

There are five steps in the strategy for building a family-based youth ministry.

Step 1—Have an Orientation Meeting with Church Leadership

Any substantial change in the ministry's philosophy and direction must be made in conjunction with the church as a whole. Don't even think about making big changes in your ministry's vision and direction without the understanding and support of the church leadership. They must buy into your vision before you implement anything. As you prepare to share your vision and thoughts on change, ask yourself the following questions:

- *What red flags might I encounter from the church leadership regarding this change? How will I address those types of concerns?*
- *What kind of impact will this change have on the church, youth ministry or parents as a whole? How can I accentuate the positive impact and mitigate the negative impact?*
- *Are there any financial implications?*
- *Does this change fit within the overall vision and direction of the church?*
- *What resources would I need to make this change possible?*
- *What hurdles and obstacles would I need to navigate in implementing this change?*

As you answer these questions, put your thoughts together in a written proposal to the church leadership. Share your vision, the possible impact, the hurdles and the benefits. The more forethought you put into the proposal, the better chance you have that the leadership will clearly understand your heart and get behind the proposed changes.

Step 2—Have an Orientation Meeting with Youth-Ministry Leadership

The next level of leadership you will need to communicate with are those who work alongside you in the youth ministry. Clear communication shows that you value and have concern for those who are partnered with you in the ministry. Just as with the church leadership, clearly communicate the proposed changes and be prepared to deal with the impact of those changes. Again, ask yourself, *What red flags might I encounter from the youth-ministry leadership?* and *How will I address these possible issues?*

When communicating to the youth-ministry leadership it is essential to keep the following in mind:

- Be careful to value youth leaders and volunteers.
- Help them understand the value of partnering with parents—that it gets parents more involved in spiritually influencing their children.
- Let them know that they are not being replaced; instead, their impact and influence will be expanded to have a positive impact on the entire family unit.
- Be sure to give them the whole picture (a big vision)—the drawbacks as well as the benefits.
- Help them see how it will impact them in their everyday ministry settings. Explain that this is not a change in what they are doing, but reiterate that it requires a shift in their mind-set from focusing just on the child to reintroducing parents into the spiritual-development equation.
- Don't forget—people support what they create. Be sure to spend some time allowing your youth leadership to interact with ideas and applications. Let them dream about how it will play out day to day. As they begin to wrap their arms around it, they will begin to own it.

Step 3—Have an Orientation Meeting with Parents

After you have shared your vision with both the church and the youth-ministry leadership, it's time to share your heart with the parents of your students. It is essential that you help them embrace the truth of Deuteronomy 6:4-9, strongly encouraging them to embark on the adventure of influencing the spiritual nurture of their children. Some parents may readily accept the challenge; others will not. Most will feel nervous about spiritually leading their children because they feel inadequate—they don't know where to begin. Reassure them that you will come alongside them with resources and support to *partner* with them. Assure them that the wonderful influence of youth ministry will continue. Again, clearly articulate what these changes will look like. This issue of partnership needs to be tangible to them.

During the meeting, inform parents of any changes that may be coming down the road. But always remember: It is better to underpromise and overdeliver than to overpromise and underdeliver. Broken promises and unfulfilled expectations undermine any change we undertake. Share from your heart, but be mindful of any expectations you may be communicating.

Step 4—Develop a Timeline for the Process

After meeting with the leadership parents, you can begin to put changes in motion. It's a good idea to put all the changes you'd like to see into a written timeline, and as your timeline rolls into motion, keep the following in mind:

- Be realistic, especially considering the impact of change and how large a change it will be.
- Consider the hurdles and the resources you have in effecting change.
- Do not move faster than is reasonably possible. The bigger the change, the more time you must give for it to sink in with all involved.
- Explain to the appropriate parties all necessary aspects of the change—perhaps finances, training, required resources, consultation and/or approvals are a concern.
- Make copies of the timeline available to church leadership, youth-ministry leadership and interested parents.
- Put the plan into action.
- Refer back to the timeline to evaluate the process of change.
- Make any changes necessary to your timeline as the changes progress.

Step 5—Begin the Process All Over Again

Once you have successfully made the changes you set out to make, take some time to reflect on the process. What worked? What didn't work? What things happened the way you expected? What was different than what you expected? If you were to go through this process again, what would you do the same? What would you do differently?

Once you have an understanding of the process and how it works in your unique church setting, find another area of family-friendly ministry that you want to see changed and go through the same process again. Continue to make the necessary changes, always looking ahead to what changes need to be made in the future. We truly believe that family-based youth ministry is not a program or a fad. It's a necessary shift in thinking in order to see students impacted more deeply than ever before. Family-based youth ministry is about bringing parents back into their spiritual-leadership roles to influence their children in positive ways. Long after the youth meetings are gone, long after middle-school and high-school events and trips are finished, long after their youth worker is out of the picture, their parents will still be there. We need to be about more than creating memories and experiences for students; we need to be about creating these things for *families*.

STRATEGY DOS AND DON'TS

Here are some things to do when changing your focus to a family-based ministry program:

- **Begin slowly and purposefully.** Allow time for one new thing to take root before moving on to another. For example, you may need to focus solely on the parents of incoming seventh graders and then let that influence grow to include the rest of the ministry over time. *It is better to be effective with a small change than ineffective with too much change.*
- **Communicate the vision in different ways.** Repetition is the key to helping people fully understand and capture your vision; you may feel like a broken record, but it is vital that you share your passion over and over again. Use natural lines of communication—newsletters, sermon messages, training opportunities, church-leadership events, and plain ol' one-on-one conversation. You may even want to bring in an expert, even if he or she is from the same city. (See pages 20-23 for more help on communicating a vision.)
- **Spend more time listening to and talking with parents.**

Throughout the process, spend time with parents, asking questions and listening to their hearts, struggles, joys and dreams. Most parents really do care and want the best for their kids. As you listen, you'll gain a clearer perspective on the issues parents face today. When I (Jim) was a younger youth worker, I found myself siding with the students most of the time when they complained about their parents. I was intimidated by parents and spent little time with them. As I matured in my approach to youth ministry, I began to listen to the people who lived with "my" kids—their parents. These people obviously had invested much more in these kids than I had. A good conversation with a parent is well worth the time and energy it takes.

- **Stay the course.** In the face of misunderstanding, don't compromise your vision. Transitioning any area of ministry can be a tough road. Have your vision clear in your own mind and do your best to convey it clearly to others. Have it in writing and refer to it often. Make sure that the vision is the lens by which you view the landscape of your youth-ministry setting. Remember the words of Proverbs 29:18: "Where there is no vision, the people are unrestrained" (NASB). Simply put: Those who aim at nothing will hit it every time.

- **Choose your battles wisely.** Your time, energy and patience are limited. Don't rush to battle unnecessarily. There will be enough necessary conflicts to face without us adding any more. When it does come time to strap on the armor (and the time will come) be sure to consider the old saying Is this the hill on which I care to die? Before marching onto the battlefield, ask yourself, *How will these people react? How will I respond thoughtfully and proactively to their concerns?*

- **Watch out for biting sheep.** Sheep are notorious for biting each other, and so it is with the Church. Often, the people who cause us the most pain are other members of the Body of Christ. Beware of people who say and do many hurtful things "in the name of Jesus." Christians are saved, but we are not yet perfect, and if you encounter biting sheep, bring in the reinforcements (your pastor, elders, other church leaders, parents and even students) to help you confront them.

We know of one youth worker who simply cancelled a Bible study and used the church bulletin to inform the congregation that the youth-ministry's philosophy and programming was changing to a more family-based approach. Some parents were up in arms over the decision and the youth pastor had to leave the church. This sad situation could have been avoided if only the youth worker had shared his vision and plan with the church leadership and the parents of the kids in his ministry. He also could have brought in the pastor and other leaders to help communicate the vision.

- **Be willing to decrease capacity for a season.** During the transition from a traditional youth ministry to a family-based ministry, your own personal effectiveness in the lives of your students may actually decrease. While this may look like a step backward, it's not. You have to allocate your time and energy toward increasing parental influence during the transition period. The dividends far outweigh the investment; think with the end in mind—not what *is* but what *could be*.

- **Have a strategic plan.** To put it simply, if your plan can be implemented in less than a year, your vision is not big enough. A strong, strategic plan will take years to develop and implement fully. It will also likely take years to see the full fruit of your efforts. You may see some immediate benefits, but the lasting ones will be developed over time.

- **Remember that the only way out of a mess is through it.** Although a human trait is to gravitate toward the well-traveled trails, transitioning a ministry means putting on your hiking boots and heading off into unknown territory where issues and hurdles abound. Take heart: When you are consciously proactive in addressing and solving problems as they come up, you can prevent them from becoming overwhelming. And, tempting as it might be, *don't* ignore issues and hope they'll go away—they won't!

Here are some things you *don't* want to do:

- **Neglect your homework.** Don't be one of those well-meaning youth workers who has a great vision but falls short of goals because you didn't do your homework. This little exercise in strategy will undoubtedly save you a great deal of potential frustration. When your game plan is communicated correctly, parents, kids and church leadership usually get it.
- **Try to change your ministry too fast.** Transitioning a traditional youth ministry to a family-based youth ministry takes time. When we move too fast, someone will always be left behind or have his or her issues left unanswered. It will take effort, but you'll have to reeducate those around you before they can make this family-based ministry idea their own. In the corporate world, this is called reengineering. In order to reengineer a program properly, you must be well prepared and ready to work out the kinks. Coming in with a lot of new changes to the ministry usually sends up red flags and makes people nervous. Slow and sure is a good motto here.
- **Assume that just because you've said it, they have heard it.** How others process what they hear is just as effective as what we say. Slow down the exchange of information to allow people to ask questions and gain the clarity they need in order to be able to support the vision. We have said it before, and we will say it again: People support what they help create.
- **Limit family-based youth ministry to a program.** If there is an overarching theme throughout this book, it is that family-based youth ministry is not about adding programs to an already full ministry plate. Instead, it is a mind-set shift that moves into every aspect of our ministry. If we limit family-based youth ministry to putting out a newsletter or having a quarterly parent event, we have missed the essence of what being family based is all about—partnering with parents to help them assume their God-given role for spiritual influence in the lives of their children.

CHAPTER FIVE

OBSTACLES TO BUILDING A FAMILY-BASED YOUTH MINISTRY

It has often been said that humankind is its own worst enemy. The battle of the mind extends into every area of our lives, and wrong attitudes can cause us to self-destruct—especially in ministry. This chapter explores five main obstacles or mentalities we may face as we transition to a more family-based approach in our ministry.

As you transition to a more family-friendly style of ministry, keep in mind that no dream of any value is accomplished without healthy doses of sacrifice, negotiation and, yes, even a few obstacles. Take the world of athletics, for example. From an early age, each athlete must make a commitment to his or her dream and decide that no matter the obstacle the dream is worth the cost. The many years of training and sacrifice that a successful athlete must endure in order to compete are quickly overshadowed by a few moments of glory after competing well in a competition.

There's an old saying that goes something like this: There's no crown without a cross. Nothing of eternal worth comes without some sacrifice. Those of us in ministry live with that truth every day, and we have experienced firsthand the setbacks and sacrifice that go into obtaining victory. Transitioning from a traditional approach to a family-based youth ministry is also not going to come without sacrifices. You're going to face enough obstacles, so don't let your own mentality be one of them. In order to see this vision become a reality, we must be committed to it—even if our commitment includes taking a hard look in the mirror at our own motivation and attitudes.

THE JUST-GIVE-ME-THE-PROGRAM MENTALITY

"Family-based youth ministry? You're kidding, right?! I can't think about parents; I'm already too busy ministering to students. I don't have any spare time to plan events for parents. Once you've got a program, I'll buy it." Sound familiar?

For years, when we thought about a more family-based approach to our youth ministry, all we could think was, *Great idea! But I don't have time to create a program.* Ask most youth workers about their ministry with parents and most will reply, "I'd love to—and I know we need to—but I just don't have the time. I'll get to it next year."

The central focus of changing your mind-set is to look through a new lens to evaluate and modify your *current* programming. For example, rather than just taking students on a retreat, a family-based ministry will take the extra step to use a retreat to influence the whole family. (See chapter 2, p. 18 for more about involving parents in retreats and camps through parent information meetings.) Sometimes (but definitely not all the time) influencing the whole family may mean changing the content of (or who participates in) the actual retreat.

Infusing a new mind-set into what we are already doing in ministry causes us to ask questions such as, What else can we do for parents and families? and How can we do what we do with more of an eye towards the building up of families?

THE I-WAS-HIRED-JUST-TO-WORK-WITH-THE-KIDS MENTALITY

When a youth worker possesses this narrow-minded mentality, he or she is assuming that kids can be pulled out of their families and ministered to in virtual isolation—and that their family lives have no impact on their spiritual well-being. While it's true that your title may say that you are the youth director, youth pastor or youth worker, you are really a minister to families. We have been given a charge to influence the spiritual lives of students, and consequently, we need to see that charge as strategically interacting with the family unit.

You were probably drawn into the field of youth ministry because you have a heart for students. Perhaps someone invested in your life when you were young, and this is your way of giving back what you received. Perhaps it's simply your passion to see the lives of young people changed as they encounter God. Whatever your reasons for being involved in youth ministry, turning your ministry into a family-based ministry does not change that. Our primary audience may be the students we see week in and week out, but healthy youth ministry says students cannot be ministered to when isolated from their families. We must work as a team with parents, teachers and other concerned adults to influence students.

THE FEAR-FACTOR MENTALITY

The year was 1989, and I (Mike) was the new guy. I was fresh out of college, long on passion and dreams but short on experience. I had just been hired as the junior high director at a church in Southern California, and I was ready to see God do big things in our midst. We were filled with ideas for ministry and programs waiting to be planned. I can still remember the day this thought came to me: *You know, I think that we should maybe have a parent meeting.* A parent meeting. Nothing truly strikes fear into the heart of a young youth worker like those words do.

My first parent meeting was an absolute disaster—more of a clinic on what *not* to do with a parent meeting. I sent out letters to all the parents, inviting them to a "parent meeting to discuss the junior high ministry." Now for a young youth worker, my idea of a parent meeting was me standing in front of a bunch of really grateful parents, espousing on the wonders of God and the junior high ministry. They would surely be gathered around, taking copious notes.

What I saw in my mind and what took place that night were two diametrical events. As the parents began to enter, I was struck with one overwhelming emotion: fear. *What on earth am I doing?* I felt completely comfortable with the junior high students, but *these* people? They were, well, they were big and old and looked like they came with an agenda (which they did).

Now don't get me wrong. Some of the parents were there to see how they could support the youth ministry. But there were others who wanted to ask *questions*—questions that, by the end of the night, I realized I had no clue how to answer. Don't get me wrong, they were great questions, and ones that I should have thought of—questions like "What's your goal for our children?" "What do you plan on teaching our kids?" "How can we be involved?" "What exactly is going on with the junior high ministry?" and "Why aren't we going to the denominational camp this year?" Without any handouts, calendars or even the beginning of a thought-out plan, I stumbled miserably through that evening and left afterward with a specific target for my overwhelming fear: parents.

It can be easy to feel intimidated when interacting with parents. For some youth workers, it's the difference in ages; for others it's the sudden realization that, as nonparents, they don't have a clue what to say! Whatever the cause for the fear, the reality is that fear paralyzes. It successfully builds walls where bridges should be built. We are partners with parents, not adversaries. Becoming a family-based ministry requires leaning into a relationship with parents based on mutual concern and care for our students—their children.

THE MY-KIDS-DON'T-COME-FROM-CHRISTIAN-HOMES MENTALITY

Gather any number of youth workers together to discuss partnering with parents and you're bound to hear "That's a good thought, but most of my students don't even come from Christian homes. What do I do about them?" or something close to it. Working with parents who know and love Christ can seem like a slam dunk; we partner with them to help them copastor their children. Where there is no spiritual foundation in the home, however, it can be tempting to abandon the idea of partnering with parents—but that is where the Body of Christ comes into play.

Family-based youth ministry is not about working exclusively with Christian families. The Church acts much like an extended family to those students who do not come from Christian homes. It provides caring Christian adults who will reach out and nurture students in their faith—this puts us in a better position to reach nonbelieving parents than the prevailing mind-set in youth ministry. I (Jim) want to share the following true story with you. How do I know it's true? Because it happened in my youth group!

> Alyssa was a sophomore at one of the local high schools. A few of Alyssa's friends invited her to one of our Sunday-morning events, and although Alyssa's mom had not stepped foot inside a church in years, Alyssa decided to come to the event. Little did she know that this was the first step in a journey that would transform not only her life but her mom's life too.
>
> Alyssa was immediately taken in by one of our adult leaders and over the course of the next few months surrendered her life to Christ. Alyssa's mom, Karen, was the first to notice a change. At first, Karen was skeptical, but as a single parent, she quickly thought to herself that a little "religion" might keep Alyssa out of trouble. Karen was distantly supportive of her daughter's involvement in the youth ministry, and because she could see that we loved her daughter, she welcomed us into Alyssa's life.
>
> Over the course of the next year, we began to reach out to Alyssa's mom. The adult leader who was working with Alyssa attended school functions and was even invited over for dinner at Karen and Alyssa's house. The leader encouraged Karen in her role as a single mom, letting her know how much we all loved and appreciated her daughter. One thing we all had in common was a concern and care for Alyssa.
>
> Slowly, Karen began sharing her life with the leader. She found that our adult leader was someone she could talk to, not only about Alyssa, but about her own life as well. An incredible door of ministry had opened. After a year of being in contact with the youth ministry, Karen decided to see what the church itself was all about, and shortly thereafter, Karen surrendered her life to Christ.

Parents are looking for partners, not replacement parents. Family-based youth ministry opens doors simply because nonbelieving parents see our care and concern for their children. While they may not understand all that we are about, they do sense our love for their children and the support we offer them as parents. As in Karen's case, it is through this common ground that God can open doors for eternity-altering conversations. Partnering with parents, both Christian and non-Christian, is an investment in the spiritual legacy of the entire family.

THE HERO MENTALITY

Let's face it: When we stepped into youth ministry, we did it in order to see lives changed, and somewhere deep inside we believe that it all depends on us. We may not verbalize it, but the thought is still there: *If I don't do my job, my students will never hear about the love of God.* It's as if we youth workers think all of heaven is looking to us to step forward at just the right time, with just the right words, to change the course of eternity for our students.

The reality is that we only have students under our care for a very short time, but they will always be under the influence of their parents. If we desire to make the deepest impact in the lives of students in the time given, we will invest in reaching and empowering the parents to have the greatest positive spiritual impact in the future.

I (Jim) was not raised in a church. My parents were good people, but neither church nor faith were a part of our lives. I became a Christian my junior year in high school, and I am so grateful for the advice my youth worker shared with me. He said, "Jim, God gave you your parents for a specific reason." There were times as a young person when I resented the lack of spiritual input from my parents, secretly wishing I had come from a family like those of some of my new Christian friends. However, my youth worker advised me to stick with my own family; he instinctively knew that my mom and dad would be the greater influence in my life. Although my parents are not necessarily my spiritual mentors, they have greatly influenced my life. After all, I don't spend Christmas with my former youth pastor, and he doesn't remember my birthday each year, but my family does. I'm so grateful for a youth worker who strove to incorporate family in his teaching, discipleship, counseling and pro-gramming, even though he had never heard the term "family-based youth ministry." I wonder if he understands the full impact he had, not only on my life, but also on the lives of my family members—all of whom now follow Christ.

THE POWER OF THE EXTENDED CHRISTIAN FAMILY

"What about those parents who are not spiritually nurturing their children?" you might ask. That's a fair question. But what if we were to ask Moses, "What about those parents who are just not doing their job of passing on the faith to their children? Who is supposed to take responsibility for them?" What do you think his response would be? It is incredibly significant that Deuteronomy 6:4 begins with "Hear, O Israel." These words were addressed to the entire nation, not just to parents. God's people have clearly been given oversight for their children, whether those children are born into their biological families or not.

The Church plays a vital role in the spiritual formation of believers and can act as an extended family to students who come from non-Christian homes. Christian families in the church (whether on staff or volunteer) are a valuable resource for assisting in the spiritual formation of a student's family by taking on the responsibility of being models for students.

"Not enough time" you say? Too much to do already? As Mark DeVries once told me (Jim), "If you will let the parents be the youth ministers that God is calling them to be, you will have time to reach the kids whose parents are not heeding that call."

In their book *Faithful Parents, Faithful Kids*, Greg Johnson and Mike Yorkey document a study of Christian adults that focused on determining the most effective faith-nurturing practices for parents. The results were alarming. There was no single, across-the-board practice that worked in even a slim majority of families. Some parents required their teenagers to attend church; others did not. Some had devotions together; the majority did not. Surprisingly few reported praying together as a family (only 15 percent). The most common faith-nurturing factor in more than 90 percent of those surveyed was that those students who continued in their faith had a half-dozen mentors present during their growing-up years.[1]

There is power in developing the extended family of Christ, and this must be a hallmark in youth ministry as we move further into the twenty-first century. In his book *Real Teens*, George Barna states that the loyalty of teenagers today "is not to an institution or a faith perspective but to the people whom they trust."[2] These young people have explored our programming. They've seen what we have to "offer" them spiritually. If we are truly to influence this generation, we must embrace a different way of looking at youth ministry. It is not about the programming. It has everything to do with spiritual formation. We must bring others into the process of spiritually forming children, realizing that both the nuclear family and the family of God have a profound impact in spiritual nurture and development.

The research is clear. If we want to make the most lasting impact in the lives of students, it will be through their parents, their families and the extended family of Christ. The way ahead, ironically, is backwards—back to the mind-set we had many years ago: "Hear, O Israel. . ."

VOICES

Every teenager, left to his own devices, will always gravitate to the oldest person he can find who will take him seriously and treat him with dignity and respect.—H. Steven Glenn, *Understanding Your Teenager*

Many parents are more intentional, better researched and more goal oriented when planning their vacations than they are in raising their children. —Paul David Tripp, *Age of Opportunity*

Kids who grew up in homes where they were regularly hugged and touched by Mom and Dad have been both more happy and more successful in life than those who were not. —Gary Smalley, *The Hidden Value of a Man*

Nothing has more power to influence a teenager's life—for good or ill—than home and family. Every youth-ministry hour spent equipping parents to nurture faith in their teenagers is like giving money to public television: Your gift is almost always doubled by a matching grant. Parents will always outinfluence even a great youth leader, so it makes sense to invest where you get the best return. —Rick Lawrence, *Trendwatch*

MENTORING

Mentoring is actually a very old concept. The word was first introduced in Homer's *Odyssey*. When Odysseus left to fight the Trojan War, he charged his trusted friend, Mentor, with the responsibility of running his household. In some ways, the words "mentor" and "discipleship" have become interchangeable. Discipleship is a character-building relationship that takes what has been given by God and passes it on to another person, who in turn does the same (see 2 Timothy 2:2). Mentoring is similar in that it develops a proactive relationship, or role model, for someone to imitate the mentor's behavior or lifestyle. Martin Luther once said, "Be a sort of Christ to one another." Paul said, "Be imitators of me" (1 Corinthians 4:16, *NASB*). These are definitely mentoring and discipleship words.

When I (Jim) was 16 years old, I made a profession of faith. As I've said before, I was not raised in a home with a strong sense of Christian faith. Frankly, it was a typical quasi-Christian home—where church was regularly attended on Easter and Christmas Eve (well, most years). If you were to ask anyone in our family, each would have claimed to be Christian. If asked why he or she claimed to be Christian, the answer would have been, "Because I'm an American."

Soon after becoming a Christian, I met a young theology student named John who became my Campus Life leader. During my first year as a Christian, he was my role model, mentor and spiritual director. He invited me to his home, and I watched him and his young wife (who was also involved in the ministry) relate and practice faith together. I doubt if he was ever taught that he was a part of my extended family, but that is exactly what he was—and still is—to me.

After graduate school, I went to work at a church where John would be my supervisor. He not only taught me how to do ministry, but his marriage was also an example, and he and his wife, Barbara, became parenting role models for Cathy and me. My relationship with my mentor reminds me that mentoring is a lifelong example of life and faith, not an assignment. It's a modeling relationship.

Youth-ministry is more about building an extended family and mentoring than we can find written in books (including our own!). As we look at the incredible influence of a student's family, we must also imitate the cry of the people of Israel for the intense need for community. While teaching a class recently, I met a dynamic youth worker named Angie Horn-Andreu. Angie, the director of high school ministry at a Christian conference center in Southern California, was raised in a very small church where she was surrounded by many mentors and an extended church family. Realizing that those relationships were key to her spiritual growth, Angie wrote the following:

The most valuable gift my parents gave me in the area of spiritual formation was their commitment to a small group of believers for more than 20 years. I grew up in a true extended family and the effect on my faith was profound. As part of a 30-member congregation for more than 15 years, I was able to grow up in a community of believers. My spiritual life was "public property." I had (and continue to enjoy) significant relationships with five adults other than my parents. These adults challenged me from childhood through adolescence. They asked me difficult questions about the friends I spent my time with, the boyfriends I dated and the choices I made. They called me to see how I was doing and why I didn't join my family for church on a given

Sunday. They celebrated with me during my junior high, high school and college graduations. Their children were my friends and their marriages my models—even when my own parents' marriage wasn't. I remember when I first brought my boyfriend, Johnny (now my husband), to meet the group. He understood that he was meeting the rest of my family. He knew their names and he understood their undeniable role in my life. They did too, and they took a sincere interest in the man I loved. One of the couples became our premarriage counselors, and the husband officiated at our wedding ceremony.[3]

You see, it really is possible for the church to provide mentors and an extended family to model a Christ-honoring life to students who may not have such a model at home. Chap Clark wrote, "[The extended family] does not dismiss or even diminish the role and responsibility of parents to raise their children in a household that serves the Lord; in fact, it strengthens and supports that role."[4] There is little chance, unfortunately, that any youth worker today has a job description that includes finding extended family and mentors for their students. Since it may be the most effective experience in a young person's faith development, maybe it should be included.

FOUR BIBLICAL EXAMPLES OF MENTORING

When we look to tailor mentoring and discipleship to the students in our youth groups, we should be familiar with four biblical methods of mentoring. No doubt there are more than four approaches to mentoring in Scripture, but the following seem to work best for family-based youth ministry:

One—Jesus and His Disciples: Being Real

A most incredible style of mentoring unfolds throughout the Gospels; basically, Jesus did life with His disciples. They ate, worked, ministered and traveled together, learning about each other's habits and lifestyles. It's not an accident that the Son of God chose mainly to influence the Twelve by simply building relationships with them while going through daily life with them.

Kids need significant adults to have relationships with. They need to do life together just as the disciples of Christ did with Him. They need to know mentors so well that they see not just the good days but the hard ones too. They need to spend enough time with them to know what they are thinking and what they would do in certain situations. I have found that some of the finest times of discipleship and mentoring take place when I take a kid on a speaking trip, go to a game or just hang out with him or her with Cathy at our house or the nearby yogurt shop. Obviously, there is not enough time to invest in deep relationships with every kid in your ministry (this is where an extended family of caring mentors comes in), but the ones most profoundly influenced will most often point back to a significant adult mentor.

Two—Eli and Samuel: Instruction in Hearing the Word of God

Although Eli was Samuel's teacher, he also had a relationship with him. Eli saw it as his calling from God to instruct Samuel personally in the ways of God, and Eli helped Samuel understand and respond to the Word of the Lord (see 1 Samuel 3).

In ministry, this can sometimes be done through what I like to call personally tailored discipleship. Personally tailored discipleship means teaching a young person (instruction) in an area of his or her life that needs attention. There was a time when I had three students, all in different stages of their spiritual growth, so I tailored my relationship for each one. I walked a new believer through the basics of Christianity, I had an open dialogue with and gave instruction about Christ-honoring relationships with the opposite sex to a student who came from a non-Christian home, and I helped the third student process and memorize the book of Philippians. In each case, my job as a discipler was to build a relationship with the student and give him or her the needed instruction that in another generation or home would have come from the student's father.

Three—Moses and Joshua: Passing On the Wisdom

As you read the biblical account of Moses and Joshua, you see from the very beginning (see Exodus 17:9) that Moses had chosen Joshua to lead the Israelites into the Promised Land. Moses took extra time with Joshua. Moses encouraged the giftedness of Joshua. Moses entrusted

Joshua with spying in the Promised Land and reporting back to him (see Numbers 13). Although Moses was definitely the mentor of the relationship, he and Joshua worked together to serve the people of Israel. Moses was proactively grooming Joshua to take the lead one day (see Deuteronomy 1:38; 31:1-8; 34:9).

We all need a Moses in our life, and we all need to be a Moses to a Joshua. The process of legacy is critical to the church and to the family. We can help parents in the church develop mentoring relationships with kids whose parents don't attend church. In this way, the mentors help the students to become the transitional generation.

Four—Paul and Timothy: Sharing Life

Paul called Timothy his son in 1 Corinthians 4:17. Timothy had other parents, but Paul took him in and treated him as if he were Paul's child. Many youth workers have a Paul-Timothy relationship with at least one person, and my family is no exception. For the past four months we have had one of our church's interns living in our home. She has shared life with us, seen us up close and personal and witnessed both our good and bad habits. As she prepares to leave our home and move into her own place, each member of our family is sad because we have all come to love her as our own. Cathy and I would trust her with our lives and the lives of our children. You can seldom have this kind of a relationship with someone unless there is a time of living under the same roof or an extended time of "doing life" together.

There are several excellent modern resources on mentoring and discipleship, including two of my favorites, *Connecting: The Mentoring Relationships You Need to Succeed in Life*[5] and *The Making of a Leader*.[6] There are five types of mentoring described in great detail in *Connecting*, but here is a basic outline for our purposes:

- Intensive Mentoring
  - √ The discipler
  - √ The spiritual director
  - √ The coach
- Occasional Mentoring
  - √ The counselor
  - √ The teacher

√ The sponsor
- Passive Mentoring
  √ Historical and contemporary teaching and books
- Peer Modeling and Mentoring
  √ Small groups
  √ Accountability peer relationships

Is it possible that the core of this next generation of youth ministry will be a mentoring or extended-family approach? Doug Fields of Saddleback Valley Community Church (home of the Purpose-Driven Youth Ministry movement) was in my (Jim's) youth group as a junior high and high school student. After high school he became an intern on our youth staff, and when I left the church to work with YouthBuilders (the National Institute of Youth Ministry, or NIYM, at that time), he took over my job as the youth pastor. The year I resigned from the Youth Specialties seminar team, Doug came on board with Youth Specialties. And even now we are back working together to serve the youth-ministry movement around the world.

It is evident that Doug and I have had many common shared experiences. There is a mutual love and respect for each other, our ministries and our families. In a recent conversation, Doug said to me, "I'm surprised at how many talks of yours I have heard and don't remember! But the hundreds of experiences, trips, lunches, fun and pain we have shared is never far from my heart." You too have an opportunity to build a spiritual development plan for each of your students. Hopefully, this plan includes their families, but even if a family is not active, perhaps your greatest legacy will be through mentoring someone God brings into your life.

Notes
1. Greg Johnson and Mike Yorkey, *Faithful Parents, Faithful Kids* (Wheaton, IL: Tyndale House Publishers, 1993), p. 249.
2. George Barna, *Real Teens* (Ventura, CA: Regal Books, 2001), p. 137.
3. Angie Horn-Andreu, "My Family, My Faith" (paper presented at the Graduate School of Theology, Azusa Pacific University, Azusa, CA, March 24, 2003), n.p.
4. Chap Clark, *The Youth Worker's Handbook to Family Ministry* (Grand Rapids, MI: Zondervan Publishing House, 1997), p. 19.
5. J. Robert Clinton and Paul Stanley, *Connecting: The Mentoring Relationships You Need to Succeed in Life* (Colorado Springs, CO: NavPress, 1992).
6. J. Robert Clinton, *The Making of a Leader* (Colorado Springs, CO: NavPress, 1998).

SECTION 2

THE
APPLICATION

PARENT MEETINGS

"Parent meeting"—these two little words can conjure up myriad dark and scary images. Some youth workers immediately think of the frustration they've felt after planning a great parent information meeting, only to have three moms show up (and they were the ones who already knew what's going on in the group anyway). Others imagine a nervous young youth worker standing in front of a group of parents who would much rather be somewhere—anywhere—else.

ESSENTIALS FOR EVERY PARENT MEETING

Contrary to popular belief, parent meetings do not have to be the church equivalent of being sent to the principal's office. Parent meetings can be characterized by building support, developing vision, seeing partnership strengthened and fostering ministry. Success is all in the eyes of the beholder. In order to keep your parent meeting from being a self-fulfilled prophecy of personal doom, here are a few essentials for every parent meeting:

- **Serve chocolate-dipped strawberries.** OK maybe you don't literally have to go through the time and expense of dipping strawberries in chocolate, but whatever you do, honor parents with quality. From the food you serve to the program itself, honor the parents and let them become your best marketing department for the future. (By the way, Cathy and I

[Jim] actually have served chocolate-dipped strawberries as a way of saying, "This is a special meeting. We're grateful for your time.")

- **Keep 'em laughing.** We aren't suggesting a guest appearance by a cast member from *Saturday Night Live*, but we do believe your parent meeting will be more effective if parents actually enjoy themselves. You can incorporate humor with a short video, a fun game, a lively mixer or whatever you think will help them have a memorable and enjoyable experience.
- **Remember that information is the key.** Parents love information. Have on hand plenty of copies of schedules of activities, special seminar dates and even articles by experts on parenting subjects. (Write any parenting magazine in the world, and they'll gladly send you a box of free copies.) When the parents leave the meeting they should know you and your ministry plan a little better, and they should feel that their time spent was worthwhile. Still not getting the picture? Spend an evening at a local school's open house and see for yourself the wonderful atmosphere that's been created for the parents.

ELEMENTS OF A SUCCESSFUL PARENT MEETING

Do you want to have the best parent meeting that you possibly can? Of course you do! Here are some important elements to ensuring that your parent meeting will be all you want it to be:

- **Begin with a plan.** Take the time to plan and program for your parent meeting as you would a youth event. Think through the details of the meeting—beginning, middle and end. Plan time in your schedule for affirming parents. How do you want people to feel when they enter? What kind of information do you need to communicate or discussion do you need to foster? How can you send them out refreshed and revitalized in their role as parents and in their relationship with the youth ministry? If you take the time and the effort to plan, it shows.

- **Share your vision.** Parents need to hear about the direction and vision of the youth ministry. Parent meetings can be a place to dream and get real-time feedback from parents. We can't say it enough: People support what they create. Sharing your heart and vision with parents creates ownership on their part. They begin to see themselves in the big picture and feel a part of the vision and direction. When parents see what is coming, they feel a sense of ownership that directly corresponds with their support of that vision.

- **Listen to the needs of the parents.** Parents want to feel listened to. Although one element of a parent meeting is for you to express to parents the needs of the ministry, it is equally (and maybe even more so) important to *listen*. Create a platform where parents can share what is going on in their lives and the lives of their family members. Parents want to know that the youth ministry truly cares about their needs as parents, as well as those of their children. The discussions that result from this sharing can provide insight into the family, which will help the ministry do its job better.

- **Allow time for parents to connect with one another.** Parents need to hear from other parents, to meet other parents who are going through what they are and to meet others who have already successfully navigated the waters they are in the midst of treading. Parent meetings need to be places where we can broker relationships, connect parents with others and encourage them in their primary roles in the lives of their children. Far more than a regurgitation of information on the ministry, parents are strategic places of ministry.

- **Let parents hear from everyone in the youth-group leadership.** Parents want to know who is spending time with their kids. Instead of one or two representatives from the youth ministry hosting the parent meeting, these meetings can be forums in which all of the youth workers in your ministry can meet the parents of students in their group. As they build relationships, parents will begin to see the youth leaders as people who are committed to their children because they love them and care about their spiritual growth. Once I

(Jim) started a parent meeting by simply saying, "I love your children. I promise you I will pray for them by name on a regular basis." I was amazed as I watched a few parents wipe tears from their eyes! Oftentimes the connections made between youth leaders and parents at a parent meeting reap incredible dividends down the road.

- **Pray.** Nothing cements parents and youth workers like calling on the name of the Lord together. Prayer is not what we do before we begin and at the end of our ministry time—it is the work of the ministry. Rather than using our valuable time in a parent meeting by endlessly going over details, put the details in handouts and spend quality time in prayer over the details and the ministry they represent. Praying together breaks down walls, builds bridges and unites hearts and minds. Praying together will powerfully impact people and meet their needs.

WHAT A PARENT MEETING AGENDA LOOKS LIKE

Now that we've talked about the essentials and the elements of successful parent meetings, let's take a look at what an effective parent meeting agenda might actually look like.

YOUTH MINISTRY PARENT MEETING AND POTLUCK DINNER
SUNDAY, JANUARY 12, 2003
6:00 P.M. TO 8:30 P.M.

5:00 P.M. Setup
- Dinner prepared and set up by parent volunteers (organized through the Parent Advisory Board)
- Information table set up with brochures, volunteer sign-up lists for summer events, copies of past parent e-mail newsletters and updates
- Welcome table set up with name tags and handouts for the evening
- Resource table set up with new parenting resources

6:00 P.M. Dinner

- Welcome and information tables manned with youth leaders
- Resource table with new parenting resources, overseen by youth leaders
- Discussion questions on each table as connection starters for parents:
  What was your favorite summer vacation?
  What did you like to do during the summertime?
  What was your favorite memory of the summer months?
  What does your family do now for the summer?

6:45 P.M. Introduction

- Youth leader introduces him- or herself and gives a glimpse of what to expect from the evening
- Youth worker leads opening prayer
- Youth leader highlights what is provided on the different tables

6:50 P.M. Stories

- Intro with slide show or PowerPoint presentation of volunteers in action or some multimedia from previous months of ministry
- Youth leaders share about their involvement in the ministry and tell some stories from the front lines of youth ministry

7:00 P.M. Summer Ministry Vision

- Youth leader(s) share the vision for the summer, including theme and events
- Highlight (not line by line on each page) information given to parents regarding summer events—particularly theme and major points of summer ministry

7:30 P.M. Small-Group Interaction

- Parents and youth leaders break off into small groups to discuss summer ministry and specific needs of families
- Parents break into groups to meet with specific leader working with their child
- Parent volunteer facilitates group discussion with questions provided on sheet at each table

7:50 P.M.   Prayer
- Parents and youth leaders gather together in large group for 30 minutes of prayer time, either guided by youth leader or left open

8:20 P.M.   Send-Off
- Youth leader closes presentations with any final information, again pointing out information on resource tables
- Thanks given to everyone involved in meeting; give award to parent volunteer for all he or she has done to serve youth ministry
- Youth pastor invites parents to provide e-mail and/or mailing address for newsletters and updates regarding ministry and events

8:30 P.M.   Parent Connection
- Conversation time for parents and youth workers to connect on personal level

9:00 P.M.   Cleanup
- Parent volunteers and youth workers clean up

OTHER PARENT-MEETING IDEAS

- **Bring in an expert to speak to your group.** This could be someone inside your church, a parent or someone outside your church, such as another youth worker or a parenting expert.
- **Have a Parents Panel night.** Gather a group of parents to sit on a panel and discuss issues related to parenting.
- **Have a Student Panel night.** Gather a group of students to talk about current youth culture or particular issues facing students in your area or church.
- **Have a parent share his or her story.**
- **Have students serve dinner to their parents.**
- **Have an evening committed to prayer for families and the ministry.**
- **Form parent-support groups out of the small interaction groups.**
- **Have a parent review a new parenting resource and share his or her**

thoughts with the group. (This could be done in writing as a part of the parent e-mail newsletter.)

- Distribute a list of helpful websites relating to youth culture, parenting, etc. (This could also include a listing of other family resources.)

CHAPTER EIGHT

PARENT RETREATS

One of the many ways we can assist parents in their God-given responsibility to pass on the legacy of faith to their children is by putting on an annual (or biannual) retreat just for parents. Let's take a look at an outline for a parent retreat we've titled "Influencing Your Child's Spiritual Values." First, let's look at the outline for the main points of the retreat.

ELEMENTS OF A RETREAT

THE MAIN OUTLINE

The main outline is where the bullet points of the retreat are written down. This is where you give a general overview of the reason for the retreat and what the theme is. The following is a sample of what an outline should look like:

"INFLUENCING YOUR CHILD'S SPIRITUAL VALUES" PARENT RETREAT OUTLINE

Topic

Influence of parents

Key Verses

"Hear, O Israel: The LORD our God, the LORD is one. Love the LORD

---

your God with all your heart and with all your soul and with all your strength. These commandments that I give you today are to be upon your hearts. Impress them on your children. Talk about them when you sit at home and when you walk along the road, when you lie down and when you get up. Tie them as symbols on your hands and bind them on your foreheads. Write them on the doorframes of your houses and on your gates" (Deuteronomy 6:4-9).

The Big Idea

To give parents an opportunity to connect with one another and to discuss practical ways in which to influence the spiritual values of their children.

Retreat Aims

During this retreat, you will help parents to
- Examine six compass points for directing the influence of their children's spiritual values
- Discover, through the power of connecting with other parents, the places of need within their family to foster their children's spiritual growth and value development
- Implement a plan to build a spiritual legacy and a platform to influence their children's spiritual values

LOCATION, LOCATION, LOCATION

Depending upon the size of your group, a retreat facility, cabin, hotel or camping facilities can be used. If you just can't get the parents to leave town for a night, the church is another option, but we have found it very advantageous to get the parents away from their daily grind. Be sure that you have plenty of viable breakout space for discussion groups.

TIME FRAME AND SCHEDULE

Our "Influencing Your Child's Spiritual Values" sample retreat is designed to begin on a Friday evening and end Sunday morning. You could also adapt a retreat of this type to a Friday evening through Saturday evening format.

Here is the schedule for the duration of our sample retreat:

"INFLUENCING YOUR CHILD'S SPIRITUAL VALUES" SCHEDULE

Friday

7:00	P.M.	Check-in at retreat center
8:00	P.M.	Session One
9:00	P.M.	Discussion groups
10:00	P.M.	Late-night options

Saturday

8:00	A.M.	Breakfast
9:00	A.M.	Session Two
10:00	A.M.	Discussion groups
11:00	A.M.	Free time
12:00	P.M.	Lunch
1:00	P.M.	Free time
6:00	P.M.	Dinner
8:00	P.M.	Session Three
9:00	P.M.	Discussion groups
10:00	P.M.	Late-night options

Sunday

8:00	A.M.	Breakfast
9:00	A.M.	Session Four
10:00	A.M.	Discussion groups
11:00	A.M.	Dismissal

When scheduling free time or late-night options, be sure to offer a listing of activity options for the specific area of your retreat. It can be helpful to recruit some volunteers to oversee and organize these options. For example, you might have one volunteer couple oversee the free time and have them organize other couples to oversee and plan the individual options. Here are some ideas:

- Taking a long walk together
- Reading

- Going to the movies together (depending on the location of the retreat facility)
- Shopping
- Bowling
- Playing broom hockey (This is great if the parents in your group are really adventuresome. Try videotaping them, so you can show the video to your students when you get back!)
- Playing a board game
- Participating in recreational games (volleyball, badminton, swimming, etc.)
- Napping (Trust us—parents will love this option!)
- Exploring any local traditions or activities

TEACHING CONTENT

Although the teaching component is vital to a parent retreat's success and effectiveness, it is not the main thrust of the retreat. The true effectiveness of any retreat lies in the quality of the discussion groups and the territory they cover (or uncover). Our sample retreat is built around six compass points—six vital elements for a healthy home environment that will foster discussion and the transfer of spiritual values. The idea is to present these six compass points in a large group and then unpack them in the smaller, more intimate discussion groups. Let's take a look at what an outline should look like.

"INFLUENCING YOUR CHILD'S SPIRITUAL VALUES" SESSION OUTLINES

Session One

Divide parents into groups of four and have them discuss: **Who or what are some of the things influencing children today?** After a few minutes of discussion, invite volunteers to share their insights. After they've shared, use play dough to mold a sculpture, giving parents a visual demonstration as you discuss the influences that are molding children today.

- Read Deuteronomy 6:4-9 as a group. As a goal-oriented society that uses everything from simple to-do lists to sophisticated PalmPilots, we want to quantify everything. But there's no set formula that says "Do these five or eight things and your children will love God." The Bible does say that we are to love the Lord our God with all that we are. Do we love the Lord our God with our whole being? You cannot impart or give what you don't have. When we love God like that, we will naturally teach that type of relationship with God to our children—and others.
- Read Proverbs 22:6. Training up a child means guiding, directing, forming, molding, shaping, encouraging and modeling what is right. (Emphasize that this verse is not a promise but a guideline.)
- Read Proverbs 4:10,20; 5:1; 6:20; 7:1. Children are to obey, heed, cling to and treasure the word of their parents—but they need to know what the Bible says in order to learn to do these things.

  Explain that the most valuable contribution a parent can make to a child is to instill in him or her a genuine faith in God. This is one of the most difficult tasks in parenting, according to Dr. James Dobson. Unfortunately, there are no magical techniques or formulas; you can't just run out to your local store and buy the $29.95 special.
- Read Proverbs 10:9. Integrity and excitement and passion for Christ are caught, not taught. How are we doing at leading our children? That's the bottom line. Are we leading from a place of integrity? Do our lives match the spiritual values that we desire to impart to our children?

  During this retreat, we will be looking at six compass points to help us navigate the seas as we venture toward influencing our children for Christ.

Session Two
Compass Point 1: Talk to Your Kids About God

Begin with a role-play of a parent trying to talk with his or her child about God. Choose two parents to act out the roles of parent and child. The child should press the parent with tough questions and the parent should act nervous. Let the role-play go on for a few minutes; then explain that adults have a tendency to either freeze up completely when faced with tough questions or move into "preachy" mode (what kids hear when we talk about God).

Share the following ideas for talking to kids about God:

- **Be yourself.** Let discussion be natural and conversational, and look for teachable moments. We love to plan for the future as if we'll always be here, but we never know how much time any of us will have. It is important to look for opportunities in everyday life when we can show our children who God is.
- **Grow yourself.** Kids grow when they see us grow. It's easier to talk about God when it comes naturally (see Deuteronomy 6:5).
- **Share yourself.** Share your victories, disappointments and your own story. Ask their forgiveness when you are wrong, and forgive them verbally, not just through actions. This makes you more accessible and real to your kids.

Have parents find a partner (someone other than their spouse if married) and share their answers to the following questions:

- What is your biggest frustration in talking with your kids about God?
- What is your biggest fear in talking with your kids about God?
- What is your desire in this area as a parent?

Compass Point 2: Make Life a Spiritual Adventure

It's a sin to bore kids with the gospel. This is the motto of Jim Rayburn, founder of Young Life. We need to seek to build spiritual memories with our children. One way to do this is with a family devotional time. These times can bring the Bible alive while forging comforting and pleasant memories and traditions with our children.

Share the following basic ingredients for creating a family devotional time:

- Entering into a discussion or activity together
- Opening the Word of God and discovering what it has to say
- Praying together

Divide the group into smaller groups of four and have each group brainstorm as many ideas as they can for family devotional times. Allow 15 to 20 minutes of discussion; then gather the groups back together and have them share some of the ideas they developed. At the end of the sharing, close the session by distributing copies of "Fifty-Two Family Devotional Ideas."

Session Three

Compass Point 3: Build Spiritual Traditions

Share a few of the spiritual traditions your family had when you were growing up. If you did not come from a home where those were present, ask others for examples to share.

Thanksgiving, Christmas and Easter are all great times for tradition. Some traditions build memories and foster laughter and fun; some solidify what we are teaching and training our kids; some do both. Families that build traditions also build connection and intimacy emotionally and spiritually. Ask the parents to share family traditions they had or still have.

Share the following ideas for creating memorable family traditions:

- Designate a "special" plate and use it as a tangible statement of "You are special today."
- Sing "Happy Birthday" to Jesus and read the Christmas story (Matthew 1:18-25 and Luke 2:1-20) on Christmas morning.
- Take your child to see a movie after school on the last day of school before Christmas break.
- On a child's birthday, wake him or her up by jumping on the bed while singing "Happy Birthday."
- Serve Thanksgiving meals at a local homeless shelter.
- Buy and wrap a gift for Jesus at Christmastime and then give that gift to a local charity.

Have parents find a partner (again, someone other than their spouse) and share one tradition they now have as a family and one they had while growing up. Give each pair exactly two minutes to share and then tell them to find new partners and share new traditions. After you are finished you could have a few people share great ideas they heard from others. Remind them that everyone has some traditions from the past as well as the present. The question we must ask ourselves is *How proactive am I in developing spiritual traditions within my family?*

Compass Point 4: Become Involved in Ministry as a Family
Share with parents that the call to Christ is a call to serve, and we can teach our children to serve through a lifestyle of servanthood, allowing them to watch as we serve others and allowing them to serve with us. Families that serve and minister to the needs of others together build deeper spiritual bonds.

Divide the group into smaller groups of four and have the groups brainstorm serving and ministry ideas that they can do with their children. (One great avenue is through Compassion International. You can encourage parents to check out www.compassion.com for more information.)

Session Four
Compass Point 5: Create a Desire for God's Word

Share with parents that one of the greatest things we could ever do for our children spiritually is create a desire in them for God's Word, because no matter where they go or what they experience in their lifetime, His Word will always be there. Share the following points:

- **Children need a foundation built on the Word of God.** "For, all men are like grass, and all their glory is like the flowers of the field; the grass withers and the flowers fall, but the word of the Lord stands forever" (1 Peter 1:24-25).
- **Children need to encounter the living Word of God.** "How can a young man keep his way pure? By living according to your word. I seek you with all my heart; do not let me stray from your commands. I have hidden your word in my heart that I might not sin against you" (Psalm 119:9-11).

Share the following ideas for creating a desire for God's Word in the hearts of children:

- Surround yourself with good resources to share (e.g., stories, videos, songs).
- Let your child see you reading the Bible.
- Share conversationally what God is teaching and showing you through His Word.
- Show your continual appreciation for God's Word through your thankfulness for its daily impact on your life.

Have parents partner with someone they haven't partnered with yet and share one thing God has been teaching them lately and how they can share that one truth with their child.

Compass Point 6: Be on Your Knees

Share with parents that it is imperative that we be on our knees for our kids, showing them that there is power in prayer. Read Philippians 4:6-7 and point out that prayer helps us step out of the way and let God work.

> *I don't know how, but there's power when I'm on my knees. . . . There I am before the One who changes me.*
> JACI VELASQUEZ, "ON MY KNEES"

Point out that children are not "ours"; they are gifts entrusted to our care by God in His infinite wisdom. As parents, we have been given the opportunity to raise God's children, and when you think about it this way, you can't help but humble yourself before Him on your knees, knowing you can't raise His kids without His help.

Share Philippians 1:9-11 and help parents apply this passage to their children.

- **Verse 9: "And this is my prayer: that your love may abound more and more in knowledge and depth of insight."** Abounding love means love that continues to increase greatly. Our prayer for our children is that their love for others and for God would continually deepen.
- **Verse 10: "So that you may be able to discern what is best."** Our prayer for our children is that they can discern what is best from what is just good or better.
- **Verse 10: "Be pure and blameless until the day of Christ."** Our prayer for our children is that their lives would be marked by integrity; that they would seek purity in life, relationships and motives.
- **Verse 11: Be "filled with the fruit of righteousness."** Our prayer for our children is that the results of living as God would want would be evident in their lives; that the results would equal intimacy with God, passion for Christ and the things of God, and an intimate and powerful prayer life.

Invite parents to spend the next five minutes praying specifically for their children, using Philippians 1:9-11 as a model.

SMALL-GROUP DISCUSSION STARTERS

The key to any effective retreat is the quality of the discussions—that is what people take home with them. The following are discussion questions for each session of our sample retreat. It's a good idea to type or write your questions and then make copies for discussion leaders (along with your notes from the sessions). This will provide each discussion group with more than enough content for a great discussion. At the end of each session, have the smaller groups find a quiet place to interact with the discussion starters.

"INFLUENCING YOUR CHILD'S SPIRITUAL VALUES" DISCUSSION STARTERS

Session One

1. What are some of the messages that influence our children? Who are the messengers?
2. What does Deuteronomy 6:4-9 mean to you as a parent? What does it mean for us as a church body?
3. What did you think about the quote from Dr. James Dobson? Is he correct? If so, what keeps us from proactively pursuing that goal?
4. What do integrity and parenting have to do with each other? What does integrity in parenting look like? What areas do you need to work on?
5. What are you looking for during your time at this retreat?

Session Two

1. When you talk to your kids about God, what is the conversation like? What kinds of things do you talk about?
2. What is your biggest frustration in talking with your kids about God?

3. What is your biggest fear in talking with your kids about God? What are some ways in which you can overcome those frustrations and fears?
4. Which area do you think is needing the most attention (e.g., being yourself, growing yourself, sharing yourself)?

Session Three

1. What are some spiritual memories you have of your childhood? What are some of the ones you've enjoyed with your kids?
2. What are some spiritual traditions you have as a family? (Going to church as a family is a great tradition!)
3. What are some roadblocks that keep you from serving and ministering together as a family?
4. What are some ideas we (youth workers) can implement in serving and ministering together as a family?
5. Families that serve together create a lifestyle of servanthood. How have you seen this statement be true?

Session Four

1. How have you seen God's Word impact your life?
2. What are some practical things you've tried to create a desire for God's Word in your children?
3. What do you pray for your children? What do we need to be praying for them?
4. Which of the six compass points do you need to give the most attention to this next month? What is one thing that you can do to focus on that area?

Well, that's it! Now that you know what a parent retreat should look like, you can start thinking about your own. You can use guest speakers, find a great video curriculum, do your own thing or adapt a ready-made outline. (Note: You're welcome to adapt our sample retreat for your own use.)

FIFTY-TWO
FAMILY
DEVOTIONAL
IDEAS

Many Christian parents really *do* want to have family devotional times with their children. Some just need help with some resources and a little coaching from you. The missing ingredient may be as simple as a few creative ideas to get them started. That's what this chapter is all about. The following pages are reproducible. Some of these ideas work better with teens and some with younger children. We've tried to include ideas that are appropriate for all ages.

When you have the opportunity to encourage parents in this area, remember that more often than not, parents feel intimidated by the idea of family devotional times. They fear they don't have the creativity, time or knowledge needed to lead their family spiritually. The key is to challenge the parents to do *something*. Encourage them to keep devotional times shorter rather than longer and to make the times experiential— this is not a time to discipline or lecture the kids. We also suggest you develop a resource library for parents in your church on this specific subject. (Each reproducible section has a list of our three favorite sources for helping to make family time great.)

FAMILY DEVOTIONAL IDEAS

ACTIVITIES THAT INSPIRE

A NIGHT AT THE MOVIES

With so many great Christian children's videos available, we would be remiss not to use them. From *VeggieTales* (with teenagers Bob the Tomato and Larry the Cucumber) to *Adventures in Odyssey* and *The Story Keepers*, there are many quality video resources to use as a family. Be sure that you preview the video for its themes before showing it to your children, so you're better prepared to guide a discussion afterward.

ATTEND A WORSHIP SERVICE

It is amazing how many families go to church together but never worship together as a family. The adults go to "big church" and the kids attend Sunday School. That's not necessarily a bad thing, but make it a point to attend a worship service together as a family, even if it's a once-a-month tradition. After the service, take your kids out to lunch and talk about the service and what impact the experience had on each of you.

LIGHTS, CAMERA, ACTION!

It's one thing to read a Bible story together, but it's another thing to see that story come to life. The next time you're tempted to just read the story—don't! Assign your children to various characters in the "script" and have them act out the story while you read it aloud. Depending on their ages, a little poetic license must be granted. Allow them to come up with their own dramatic interpretations of how the story would have been lived out. The results are sure to be both hilarious and insightful.

FAMILY TRUST WALK

Remember this youth-ministry classic? Why not do it as a family? Pair off and blindfold one person in each pair. Have the other person lead them around the house using their voice—no touching—to guide them. After a tour of the house, have each person share about their experience and how it relates to their relationship with God and trusting Him.

HAVE A WORSHIP SERVICE IN YOUR HOME

For a change of pace, have a worship service in your home—complete with singing, Scripture reading and a devotional (preferably led by one of the kids). This will not only model the biblical truth that we are all ministers, but it will also give the members of your family a greater appreciation for one another and the gifts God has given them.

MEMORIZATION MADNESS

At the beginning of the year, find a handful of verses that you'd like to memorize as a family. Write them out on pieces of blank paper, note card or sections of poster board. Find a place to post the verses, preferably in a place where everyone will see them (e.g., the kitchen or dining room). Routinely introduce a new verse, as well as review past verses. You can make a game of it by initially posting them in hidden places for the family to try and find. You can also add incentives for memorizing the verse the fastest, knowing the most verses, etc.

ROAD TRIP

Why talk about a living truth in a sterile environment? Jesus took the disciples to places where they could see, taste and touch the truth. Instead of having a devotional at home, find an environment that will better help your family see, taste and touch the truth. If you are going to talk about life and death, go to a cemetery or a mortuary. If you are going to talk about the busyness of life, take them to a mall or an airport during the Christmas or any other holiday season.

SHOOTOUT AT THE OK CORRAL

This devotional is best for the summertime or warmer climates. Arm each member of your family with squirt guns, water balloons, hoses, water cannons, etc. Then let the gunslinging begin! At the end, gather together and talk about Jesus' statement that He is the *living water* that can satisfy our thirst (see John 4:10). Explore this truth with questions. What is the role of water in our lives? How does Jesus come to us as living water? Where are we thirsty and in need of His living water in our lives?

STAKING A CLAIM

As a family, go to your local hardware store and buy a wooden stake. Write out Joshua 24:15 on the stake and discuss what it means to claim that you and your family will serve the Lord. Family members can write what this verse means to them somewhere on the stake and then you can take the stake outside to your front lawn and drive it into the ground (letting everyone take turns pushing it down to set it firmly) to make the claim that your house is a place where God is exalted and will be served.

Online Resources for Family-Time Tips

For helpful information on making time with your family more meaningful and influential, check out the following Internet sites:

- **Heritage Builders (www.HeritageBuilders.com)**—A ministry of Focus on the Family, Heritage Builders exists to help families with family times. It would be well worth your time to check out their outstanding materials.
- **YouthBuilders (www.YouthBuilders.com)**—Check out our online store and search under "family devotions" for a list of our favorite family devotional books. You'll also find some more ideas for devotionals on our website.
- **Big Idea Foundation (www.bigideafoundation.org)**—From the creators of *VeggieTales* comes an entire website devoted to great devotional ideas and object lessons. The Big Idea Foundation recognizes the profound impact time together has on families and has used their creativity to make those times fun as well.

FAMILY DEVOTIONAL IDEAS

GOING DEEPER—GREAT DISCUSSION STARTERS

AFFIRMATION BOMBARDMENT

Read Hebrews 10:24-25 as a family. Give each member of the family one piece of paper for every other family member (e.g., if your family has four people, each person will receive three pieces of paper) and something to write with. Each person should write three affirming words or phrases about another member of the family on each piece of paper. When everyone is finished, share what everyone has written and then give each family member the papers that affirm him or her.

AFFIRMATION NOTES

Write notes of encouragement to the other people in your family, expressing what you appreciate about them. Attach any verses that come to mind as you think about each person and what he or she means to you.

ALPHABET OF THANKFULNESS

Read 1 Thessalonians 5:18 as a family, and then play a fun twist on the alphabet game. Starting with the letter A, think of one specific reason to be thankful and continue around the family until the entire alphabet has been used. Write each reason on a huge piece of butcher paper and hang it in a prominent place in your house where everyone can be reminded of what to be thankful for. This is especially good for those nonthankful days all smaller children have at one time or another.

ANSWER THIS!

Have each person in your family create five open-ended statements on slips of paper; then fold the papers and put them in a hat. One at a time, have family members pull out a piece of paper and complete the statement. Keep going until all the statements have been completed. Here are some sample statements:

- The time I felt closest to God was . . .
- The time I felt the farthest from God was . . .
- I feel encouraged when . . .
- If I could ask God one question, it would be . . .

TEACHABLE MOMENTS

Often nonfiction stories portray great truths. Find a real-life story that challenges the thinking and ethics of living. Make copies of the story and give each family member a copy. After reading the story together, discuss the implications it has in your lives as followers of Jesus. Ask questions to get the discussion started. How would you react in this situation? How should you respond to this issue as a believer and follower of Jesus?

GOD IS . . .

Have each family member come up with as many ways as they can to finish the sentence, "God is . . ." Have them write down their responses along with any Scriptures that might apply. Gather everyone's responses and make a master list of the attributes of God. Post the list in a prominent place in your home.

GOD IS LIKE . . .

Have your family sit together in a room. Look around the room and find objects that represent a character or quality of God. Share it and any verses that may apply. For example: "God is like this chair, because I can fully put my trust in Him, knowing He will be able to support me no matter what I am going through." Keep going from person to person until you run out of objects.

THE IMPORTANCE OF BEING EQUALLY YOKED

Ask someone in your family to read 2 Corinthians 6:14, which states, "Do not be yoked together with unbelievers. For what do righteousness and wickedness have in common? Or what fellowship can light have with darkness?" Then read Jenna's story and have a discussion about the questions it raises.

Jenna has been raised in a Christian home all of her life and thinks her parents are *way* too strict. Now that she's 16 years old, they're finally giving her the opportunity to date, but Jenna's last conversation with them really bugged her.

It all started when a very good-looking guy came to pick up Jenna to take her to a high school basketball game and then to the school dance afterwards. He was very polite to Jenna's parents and got her home right on time. The next day Jenna's mom asked her if her date was a Christian. Jenna immediately got defensive and told her mom that it was none of her business—he might not be a Christian, but he was very nice and she liked him a lot.

That evening Jenna's mom and dad sat down with her after dinner and said, "We want you to know we believe it is biblically correct for Christians to date only other Christians." Jenna's response was, "Mom, you married Dad before he was a Christian and then he became a believer. Isn't that a double standard?"

Here are just a couple of questions to get your family discussing this subject:

- What do you think of the way Jenna's parents handled the situation?
- If you were giving Jenna advice, what would you tell her?
- "It is biblically correct for Christians to only date other Christians." Do you agree or disagree with that statement?

PHYSICAL AND SPIRITUAL BIRTH

Bring out your family's birth certificates and baby pictures (Mom's and Dad's too!). If possible, make a phone call to your mom and dad and ask them to share the story of your birth with your kids.

After your kids hear the story of your birth, explain that you don't remember being there for any of that story. Ask them if your not remembering your birth means it didn't happen, and explain that even though you don't remember it, you are pretty sure that you really were born. Share the story of the birth of each child in the family and ask if any of them remembers being born; then read John 3:1-12 aloud. Use the following statements for discussion:

- Just as physical birth is necessary for us to live in the world, spiritual birth is necessary for us to have a relationship with God (see John 3:3).
- We weren't responsible for our physical birth and we're not responsible for our spiritual birth—they are both acts of God (see John 3:6).
- Just as we have to depend on our parents' stories of our physical birth, we have to rely on the words of Jesus for our spiritual birth (see John 3:11-13).

Discuss the events surrounding each family member's spiritual birth. Say a prayer thanking God for the spiritual birth of each member of your family (by name).

ROCK OF REMEMBRANCE

Read Deuteronomy 32:4 and Psalm 18:2 as a family. What do they say about God? How does that truth apply to your life? In the Old Testament, when the people of Israel had an encounter with God, they would build an altar of rocks to remember God's presence. Have each family member find a rock to symbolize a significant commitment to God, such as giving a specific fear or sin over to the Lord. As you share your commitments, assemble your "altar" in a visible place as a way of remembering this special time with God and the commitments made.

SING TO THE LORD A NEW SONG

Ask each family member what his or her favorite worship song is and why. Have everyone think about a worship song that they once liked but heard too much (trust us, they will have at *least* one.) Share Psalm 96:1-6, which begins, "Sing to the LORD a new song" and ask

- Why do you think it is important to sing a "new song"?
- Do you think there are any new reasons to praise God?

As individuals or as a family, write a new praise song to God (just lyrics are fine). Incorporate specifics from your lives or from Psalm 96:1-6. Explain that this doesn't mean we shouldn't sing the old songs too but that we should continually find new ways in which to express our gratitude to God for His awesome love for us!

STRING OF AFFIRMATION
Hold on to one end of a ball of string and throw the ball to a family member while saying something encouraging about that person. That person then holds the string while throwing the ball to another family member and so on, creating a web of string from one family member to the next. Make sure that everyone gets to throw the ball to each family member at least once. Talk about the web of string and how it represents the bond you have in Christ and as a family.

THANK THERAPY
Read 1 Thessalonians 5:18 together. Have each family member write 10 reasons why they are thankful on a piece of paper and then share those reasons aloud.

THE DICTIONARY GAME
To begin this game, have one person in your family randomly open a dictionary and pick the biggest word that appears on the page. He or she can either explain what the dictionary says about that word or make up a more creative definition. Each family member then votes whether or not he or she believes that the definition given is true. Continue until everyone has a chance to define a word from the dictionary and then read John 9. Begin a discussion by asking, "How was pretending to know the definition of the word in our game similar to the way the Pharisees were acting?" (They were pretending to know everything about God but didn't.)

Have family members share about a time in their life when God helped them; then offer a prayer thanking the Lord that He not only heals physically blind people, but that He also gives sight to the spiritually blind.

WHAT WOULD YOU DO?

Give each person in your family a piece of paper and something to write with. Everyone should write out a scenario that ends with the phrase, "What would you do?" These scenarios can go along with a theme for the devotional, or they can stand alone as a way to teach the truth that our faith should holistically impact the choices we make and the way we live our lives. You can make up scenarios that best fit your unique family. Here are a few examples:

- Johnny has been approached by a stranger and the person asks him a lot of personal questions. What would you do?
- A teacher at school says she does not see how any thinking person could believe in God. What would you do?
- Friends ask you to go and see a Disney movie, but when you get there, they want you to go with them to see a very sexual and violent movie with an *R* rating. What would you do?

Online Resources for Family-Time Tips

For helpful information on making time with your family more meaningful and influential, check out the following Internet sites:

- **Heritage Builders (www.HeritageBuilders.com)**—A ministry of Focus on the Family, Heritage Builders exists to help families with family times. It would be well worth your time to check out their outstanding materials.
- **YouthBuilders (www.YouthBuilders.com)**—Check out our online store and search under "family devotions" for a list of our favorite family devotional books. You'll also find some more ideas for devotionals on our website.
- **Big Idea Foundation (www.bigideafoundation.org)**—From the creators of *VeggieTales* comes an entire website devoted to great devotional ideas and object lessons. The Big Idea Foundation recognizes the profound impact time together has on families and has used their creativity to make those times fun as well.

FAMILY DEVOTIONAL IDEAS

MAKING IT TANGIBLE

ADVENT CALENDAR

Buy an Advent calendar or wreath for the next Christmas season and use it as a way to celebrate the coming of Christ into the world, as well as into your home and hearts. In the Burns home, we have a tradition of praying around our Advent calendar for specific countries and missionaries we know during the 24 days of Advent.

BIBLE GAMES

Take a trip to your local Christian bookstore and visit the youth and children's departments. Most Christian bookstores have a great selection of Bible games for various ages, so check them out and find one that would interest your family. Playing games as a family has a way of bonding you together— and as a bonus, you can learn a little about the Bible while you're at it!

DIFFERENT GIFTS AND ABILITIES

Prepare a meal that is difficult to eat without the proper silverware (e.g., steak is hard to cut with a spoon, peas are hard to scoop with a fork). When everyone is seated at the dinner table, give each member one piece of silverware from the set (i.e., one person gets only a spoon, another gets only a fork). Ask someone to try to do something for which his or her silverware does not function best. When what you have asked is obviously harder to do without the correct silverware item, ask the person with that piece of silverware to take over and complete the task. Share 1 Corinthians 12:14-18 and then discuss the following questions:

- Why is it important to recognize our place within the Body of Christ?
- What happens if we don't think our place is as important as someone else's?

• Are all the places equally important?

Ask each family member to identify something that another member does well and how he or she could use that gift to bless others. Pray together as a family, asking God to use each person's giftedness for His glory.

FINDING GOD

When we watch the sun set or climb a mountain, Romans 1:20 is very clear. But we can find God and his awesomeness in *all* things. God is with us every day. Read Romans 1:20 as a family; then send everyone on a search around the house or outside to find an object that shows one or more of God's invisible qualities. After 10 minutes, have everyone gather around the kitchen table and share how they can see God in that item. Designate these things as focal points in your home to be reminded of that, and say a prayer asking God to help you see Him in your daily life and in all things.

GOD ART

Give each member of your family a piece of paper and have everyone divide their paper into four sections; then draw each of the following pictures in a section. Afterward, ask everyone to describe their pictures and share any Scripture that may go along with them.

• Draw a picture of God.
• Draw a picture of what it means to love God.
• Draw a picture of what it means to love others.
• Draw a picture of your own relationship with God.

IN THE HANDS OF THE POTTER

Give each person in your family some play dough and have everyone mold a sculpture representing what they want God to develop in his or her life. Ask someone to find Scripture passages that talk about God being the potter and His children being the clay, and then ask each family member to share his or her thoughts and dreams while also sharing about the sculpture they've created.

MEMORY LANE

Pull out your old yearbooks from junior high or high school (yes, the ones with *that hair!*). Let your kids find your picture and read what people wrote in your yearbook (with caution, if necessary). Use the time to explain that the issues your kids face are the same ones you faced at their age—but they are facing these issues in a completely different cultural context. After all, "there is nothing new under the sun" (Ecclesiastes 1:9). Allow your kids to share their thoughts and struggles and make sure to share some of the issues you currently struggle with as well (making sure, of course, that what you share is appropriate for your children's age level).

NOW THAT MAKES *SENSE*!

Sight, sound, taste, touch, smell—God created us to experience the world around us! It's no surprise, then, that humans learn best when we experience a truth by using the senses God has given us. Instead of just talking about a particular biblical truth, find an object, food or even sound that represents it. Then incorporate that object into your family's devotional time.

OUR ROCK

For this devotional, you'll need your Bible, a rock (small enough to hold in your hands but big enough for everyone to write on), permanent markers, and glue and glitter (optional).

Gather your family in a circle and pass the rock around to each person. As each person holds the rock, ask him or her to describe it. When the rock gets back to you, share the story of when David had to hide from Saul to save his own life. Just as the cave became David's protection, the Lord is our protection. (Read 1 Samuel 19—20 beforehand, so you can paraphrase the story.) You might also take a moment to reflect upon the hardest times your family has gone through and how the Lord was your rock during those times. Then ask someone to read Psalm 18:1-3 and discuss the following questions:

- When has the Lord been your strength, shield or salvation?
- Do you trust God to protect you?
- When have you felt God's protection the most?

- Has the Lord ever used someone here on Earth as your helper?

Have each family member write their answers on the rock using the markers and glue sprinkled with glitter. The rock can be displayed in your home or given to a family or church member who is going through a difficult time.

SCRIPTURE ART

As a family, select a verse that is particularly meaningful to you. Design a piece of art using items in your house or garage that represents the verse you've chosen. Make sure that everyone in the family contributes to the artistic design. You may want to find a place in the house to show off your piece of art. If you do this on a regular basis—perhaps yearly—you'll have designed an art gallery depicting your family's spiritual journey.

STONES OF REMEMBRANCE

In the Old Testament, God's people commemorated the acts God did in their midst by building stone altars. Joshua 4 retells the story of the Israelites crossing the Jordan River. When the Lord dried up the river His people were crossing, Joshua commanded the Israelites to take stones from the middle of the river. They then built a memorial pile with the rocks to remind them of the great and mighty God who dried up the Jordan before them.

As a family, find or purchase some large rocks and build a family memorial pile. Have each family member draw or write on a few stones representing times when he or she felt God move in the midst of your family. Over time, keep adding stones to the pile. As you look at the stones, the drawings and the words, you'll be reminded of all that God has done in your family.

THE VON TRAPP FAMILY DEVOTIONAL

If you have someone in your family who is musically inclined, spend some time together as a family singing songs of praise. You can center your family worship time on a theme or choose songs that are particularly meaningful to the family. If your troop isn't musically inclined, find other creative ways to worship God together.

WRITE YOUR OWN PSALM

Read through a few psalms together as a family. Individually or as a family, write a psalm expressing your heart of thanks, your heart of disappointment or your passion for God. You may want to write these on something large enough to post in a prominent place in your home.

Online Resources for Family-Time Tips

For helpful information on making time with your family more meaningful and influential, check out the following Internet sites:

- **Heritage Builders (www.HeritageBuilders.com)**—A ministry of Focus on the Family, Heritage Builders exists to help families with family times. It would be well worth your time to check out their outstanding materials.
- **YouthBuilders (www.YouthBuilders.com)**—Check out our online store and search under "family devotions" for a list of our favorite family devotional books. You'll also find some more ideas for devotionals on our website.
- **Big Idea Foundation (www.bigideafoundation.org)**—From the creators of *VeggieTales* comes an entire website devoted to great devotional ideas and object lessons. The Big Idea Foundation recognizes the profound impact time together has on families and has used their creativity to make those times fun as well.

FAMILY DEVOTIONAL IDEAS

PRAYER TIME

CONFESSION OF SIN

According to 1 John 1:9, when we confess our sins, God forgives us and absolutely cleanses us from that sin. Gather your family outside and have everyone take a quiet moment to write out on a piece of paper (privately) any personal sins that come to mind. After everyone is done writing, they can fold their papers several times and give them to you. Without looking at them, place the folded papers in a container suitable for burning paper (e.g., a tin can or your barbecue) and then burn the papers to signify that God forgives our sins and wipes our slate clean. Afterward, have family members pray and thank God for forgiving their sins.

DECK OF PRAYER

Shuffle a deck of cards and place it in the middle of a table. Starting with one person and going in a circle (go around the circle at least a few times), turn over a card and offer a sentence prayer using the following pattern:

- Heart—A prayer of thankfulness
- Spade—A prayer confessing sin or concerning an area of needed growth
- Diamond—A prayer about a wish, a dream or a goal for the future
- Club—A prayer for your family (an area of need or a desire for the future)

FAMILY PRAYER CALENDAR

Fill in each day of your calendar for this month with people and issues for your family to pray over. Make sure that each person in the family contributes to what goes on the calendar, and then hang the calendar in a prominent place in your home. Schedule a time that you can pray daily or weekly together for the people and issues on the calendar. The key to making this idea work is finding time to pray together regularly. Praying regularly will keep you accountable for praying for what is written on the calendar and will also help you form a habit of praying together as a family.

LET YOUR CHILDREN PRAY

Yep, encourage your kids to pray—for anything, anywhere, anytime! In the Burns family, we often pray for the family in need when an ambulance or fire truck drives by. Pray for missionaries you or your church supports. Place pictures of friends and family on the refrigerator or on the bathroom mirror as reminders to lift those people up in prayer.

PRAYER TOUR IN THE CITY

Pile into the family vehicle and drive around the city in which you live. Pray for different aspects of the city—schools, law enforcement, fire and medical personnel, homeless areas, rescue missions, crisis pregnancy centers, etc. If possible, finish your prayer tour at a location where you can view the entire city. Spend some extended time in prayer over the city, asking God to move throughout the city and change the hearts of those who don't know Him.

PRAYER TOUR OF YOUR HOME

The prayer tour mentioned above can also be done in your home. Visit each room, covering the family member who typically inhabits that room. You can also view each room as symbolic of the Christian life. (Check out Robert Boyd Munger's book *My Heart—Christ's Home* to gain more ideas for this approach.)[1] Spend time in personal and group prayer in each room before moving on to the next room.

Online Resources for Family-Time Tips

For helpful information on making time with your family more meaningful and influential, check out the following Internet sites:

- **Heritage Builders (www.HeritageBuilders.com)**—A ministry of Focus on the Family, Heritage Builders exists to help families with family times. It would be well worth your time to check out their outstanding materials.
- **YouthBuilders (www.YouthBuilders.com)**—Check out our online store and search under "family devotions" for a list of our favorite family devotional books. You'll also find some more ideas for devotionals on our website.
- **Big Idea Foundation (www.bigideafoundation.org)**—From the creators of *VeggieTales* comes an entire website devoted to great devotional ideas and object lessons. The Big Idea Foundation recognizes the profound impact time together has on families and has used their creativity to make those times fun as well.

Note
1. Robert Boyd Munger, *My Heart—Christ's Home* (Downers Grove, IL: InterVarsity Press, 1986).

FAMILY DEVOTIONAL IDEAS

SERVING AS A TEAM

SERVICE PROJECT

One thing is certain: Families that find creative ways to serve together have a richer spiritual connection as a family unit. Don't let your family miss out on this incredible experience! Perhaps you could serve at a rescue mission or a homeless shelter during the holidays—or any other time of the year. Or maybe your family can get involved in a mission experience through your church. Short on ideas? Just ask a pastor what opportunities are available. There is never a shortage of venues in which to serve others!

SERVE TOGETHER AT YOUR CHURCH

It's important for children to understand the value of the Body of Christ. Serving together at your church will help your children feel a greater bond with the congregation and allow them to taste the joy of serving other members. Your family could volunteer for an all-church workday, or maybe the children's ministry needs extra help. Serving is a unique way to bond together as a family, and it allows each member to see the influence your family can have as a unit.

RANDOM ACTS OF KINDNESS

Have each family member create a list of random acts of kindness he or she could do in the next month for someone in his or her daily life. Encourage everyone to schedule a time to do those random acts without letting the recipients know what is being done for them.

IMMEDIATE RANDOM ACTS OF KINDNESS

For a more adventuresome version of random acts of kindness, come up with a list of *immediate* things you can do to bless someone. Choose one act from the list and do it immediately. This will not only show your kids that there are those in need all around them but also how easy it can be to bless someone with a simple act of kindness.

HOMEMADE GIFTS FOR THE HOLIDAYS

Instead of buying elaborate gifts for others, make homemade gifts as a family for extended family and friends. The Burns family specialty is pumpkin bread and homemade barbecue sauce (not together, though!). For that personal holiday touch, put your gifts in a box and take them to the recipients as a family. Spend a few moments with each recipient praying God's blessings over them.

SPONSOR A COMPASSION CHILD

If you haven't done so already, consider making a sponsored child part of your family. Sponsoring a child can be an integral teaching tool and heartwarming experience. You can take time in your family devotionals on a regular basis to write and pray for your sponsored child. (For more information on sponsoring a child through Compassion International, visit www.compassion.com.)

THE ENCOURAGEMENT PROJECT

As a family, choose someone who needs a little encouragement. This person can be an extended family member, a neighbor, someone from your church or anyone else who needs a little boost. Brainstorm together and come up with an idea to bring joy to that person's life, and then spend your family devotional time carrying out that idea. My (Jim's) family decided to write notes of encouragement to a woman who had lost her husband a year earlier.

YOU ARE SPECIAL TODAY

On each family member's birthday, devote the day especially to him or her. You could take part of the day to do that person's favorite activity, spend time affirming him or her or share Scriptures that remind you of that special person. One family bought a plate that had "You Are Special Today" written on it, and the honoree got to eat all their meals on it that day. (This activity doesn't have to be limited to birthdays. You can even pick a new family member to honor each month.)

THE CHECKBOOK

Get out your checkbook and write a check for 1 million dollars, leaving the name blank. (This will no doubt leave little in your checking account!) Pass the check around and have each family member share what he or she would do with that much money. When everyone has shared, take a vote to choose the top five ideas and discuss what effect those five things would have on other people for eternity.

Ask someone to read John 11:57—12:11 aloud and then discuss the following questions:

- How did the money Mary used to buy the perfume she put on Jesus' feet make a difference? (It became a lesson for everyone who reads the Bible. She honored her Savior and many others.)
- Did the 30 pieces of silver that Judas received for turning Jesus in do him any good?

Pray that God would use your family and finances to make an eternal difference. Ask Him to show your family a ministry that they can take ownership in, where they can serve together. You could support a child in a foreign country, serve at a local soup kitchen or work together on a project at your church.

Online Resources for Family-Time Tips
For helpful information on making time with your family more meaningful and influential, check out the following Internet sites:
- **Heritage Builders (www.HeritageBuilders.com)**—A ministry of Focus on the Family, Heritage Builders exists to help families with family times. It would be well worth your time to check out their outstanding materials.
- **YouthBuilders (www.YouthBuilders.com)**—Check out our online store and search under "family devotions" for a list of our favorite family devotional books. You'll also find some more ideas for devotionals on our website.
- **Big Idea Foundation (www.bigideafoundation.org)**—From the creators of *VeggieTales* comes an entire website devoted to great devotional ideas and object lessons. The Big Idea Foundation recognizes the profound impact time together has on families and has used their creativity to make those times fun as well.

CHAPTER TEN

TRIED-AND-TRUE PARENT-SEMINAR IDEAS

Hosting parent seminars on a regular basis is a great way to assist parents. The good news is you (usually) do not have to be the speaker. More good news is that if you develop a parent-advisory group for seminars, they can do the work as long as you steer them in the right direction. We have found that parents enjoy the idea of an occasional seminar and will participate as long as they understand the value of their time investment. In this chapter, we've listed our 12 favorite topics. Some are more spiritually oriented than others, but all have been successful. We have found that even non-Christian parents show an interest in seminars that offer to help them with their relationship with their kids. Always keep in mind this thought: When you reach the family, you reach the world.

SEMINARS THAT WILL KEEP THEM COMING BACK

HOW TO HELP YOUR KIDS GET A COLLEGE SCHOLARSHIP

The attendance for this seminar has historically been one of the highest experienced by youth groups around the United States. There is a universal need and desire to learn more about helping children not only get into college but pay for it too. Bring in experts from a local Christian college as well as a Christian leader in a secular school. Ask them to make presentations, but leave lots of room for the incredible amount of questions the parents will ask (and they *will* ask). You may want to hand out devotionals on an important topic related to the subject. (By the way, be prepared to have parents of even very young kids show up to this one.)

DRUGPROOF YOUR KIDS

Studies show that over 85 percent of Christian high school students will have had a drink of alcohol by the time they graduate and a majority of teens will also have used another illegal drug.[1] Armed simply with those statistics and the overwhelming need for parents to be educated on this important subject, we recommend making it a priority to help educate parents about teen drug and alcohol use. Unfortunately, many parents are either in denial or ignorant that their children are much more susceptible to drug and alcohol abuse than they think. YouthBuilders has a great video seminar available called *Drugproof Your Kids*. For more information, visit www.YouthBuilders.com.

HOW TO TALK TO YOUR KIDS ABOUT SEX AND SEXUALITY

Yikes! In a recent seminar, I (Jim) told about 400 parents that only 10 to 15 percent of their children say they received good, positive, healthy, value-centered sex education from home. Then I asked how many of them had received healthy sex education when they were growing up. Four hands went up. We rest our case—parents need help.

ENERGIZING YOUR CHILD'S SPIRITUAL LIFE

This is the core of our Christian existence, yet far too many parents leave the spiritual direction and guidance to circumstance and chance. Armed with what you have learned in this book, we recommend you give the parents a proactive seminar focused on how to take back the God-given responsibility of building a spiritual legacy for their family.

BUILDING HEALTHY MORALS AND VALUES

One of the primary tasks of Christian parenting is to instill morals and values into the lives of our children, and this topic is always a good draw. Parents aren't interested in negative statistics and general criticism of today's society. Make sure your speaker is someone who will give practical answers and biblical solutions to the moral dilemmas facing kids today.

UNDERSTANDING THE YOUTH CULTURE
Parents must become students of the culture. This seminar would help parents understand more about the culture their kids are exposed to—especially in the areas of media, Internet and music and their influences on youth. We suggest you find a culture expert for this presentation, but if you can't find one in your local area (and you don't feel equipped to lead it yourself), you can use one of the excellent video presentations available on youth culture. Our favorite resources are the book *Understanding Today's Youth Culture*,[2] the videos *True Lies* and *Music to Die For*,[3] the magazine *Plugged In*[4] and Al Menconi's Internet website, www.almenconi.com.

KIDS IN CRISIS
It's critical to help parents understand that *prevention* of crisis is the most critical issue—particularly those parents who might be considering not attending this seminar because they don't think their kids are in a crisis. Topics such as suicide prevention, sexual abuse and satanism, along with the regular topics of sexual promiscuity and drugs, can make for a very interesting and informative seminar.

CONSISTENT DISCIPLINE
Positive, consistent discipline is a critical need for kids of all ages. When you look through the parenting section of any bookstore, you will notice a sundry of books on the subject of discipline and behavior. There is a reason for this! Parents recognize they need help in this area. Sometimes you can put on a very effective seminar with a local Christian counselor as the speaker, providing parents with excellent tools for creating healthy expectations, consequences and discipline.

COMMUNICATING WITH YOUR KIDS
Communication is key in any relationship. If you can create a seminar for parents to communicate more effectively with their kids, you will have a successful seminar. Throughout the years, this seminar is one of the most requested from YouthBuilders. Youth workers are constantly

asking how they can help parents communicate with their kids and vice versa. Given the right speaker, you may be able to combine the students and the parents in the same seminar for this topic.

MARRIAGE SEMINAR

One of the finest things parents can do for their kids is to work on their own marriage. Marriage seminars sponsored by the youth-ministry department have proven very successful; they have a way of reminding parents that their marriage directly impacts their parenting. There are usually excellent marriage communicators available to speak, but if you can't find one and you want to use a video series, we recommend Gary Smalley's *Keys to Loving Relationships* and *Secrets to Lasting Love*.[5]

BUILDING A HEALTHY SELF-IMAGE

One of the keenest felt needs of parents is helping their children develop a positive self-image. Poor self-image is at the root of many other problems kids go through. Make sure that your speaker gives a biblical perspective of a proper self-image and makes the session practical with huge take-away value. Be sure the discussion includes those things that block a healthy self-image, as well as ways to build up a shaky self-image.

TEACHING YOUR CHILDREN HOW TO HANDLE FINANCES

Most parents know they have not done an adequate job of helping their children become good stewards of their finances. Many young married couples say one of their major worries is that they were not sufficiently prepared to handle finances. This is a great tool to help parents do a more effective job of teaching their kids to be good stewards of what God has given them. A Christian financial planner or an organization like Crown Ministries could be your best resource for an excellent seminar. (For more information, visit crownministries.com.)

ORGANIZATIONS YOU CAN HIRE

If you can't find local experts to speak at your seminars, there are several national organizations that do a great job at a reasonable price. If you are a small church, the cost could become prohibitive—especially for travel—so you may want to team up with a couple of other churches in your area to bring the expert to your location. Often these organizations help you market your program, so all you need to do is charge the parents in your group a small fee.

TRAITS OF A HEALTHY FAMILY SEMINARS

These seminars by YouthBuilders are 2 ½ hours long each and very modestly priced. The topics range from "Building Healthy Morals and Values" to "Energizing Your Kid's Spiritual Life." For more information, visit www.youthbuilders.com.

UNDERSTANDING YOUR TEENAGER SEMINARS

Wayne Rice, cofounder of Youth Specialties, has created a very fast-paced, informative seminar on understanding the unique world of teenagers. As with anything Wayne does, the presentation is outstanding and every speaker is top-notch. For more information, visit www.uyt.com.

LIFE SKILLS FOR AMERICAN FAMILIES SEMINARS

Tim Smith brings us some very practical and excellent material for parents. His seminars are great learning experiences and very much appreciated by those who have experienced one of several options he provides. For more information, visit www.40days.org.

STRONG FAMILIES IN STRESSFUL TIMES SEMINARS

John Trent is one of America's finest seminar leaders on the family. We love the message and the messenger. For more information, visit www.strongfamilies.com.

PARENTING TEENAGERS FOR POSITIVE RESULTS VIDEO OR SMALL-GROUP SEMINARS

This series is by Jim. The goal is to have this video/small-group curriculum in over 10,000 churches by 2005. The following are some of the topics included:

- Attitude Is Everything
- Self-Image Struggles

- Communicating with Your Kids
- Navigating Sexuality
- Developing Media Discernment
- Helping Your Teenager Grow Spiritually

Notes

1. Steve Arterburn and Jim Burns, *Drugproof Your Kids* (Ventura, CA: Regal Books, 1995), p. 15.
2. Walt Meuller, *Understanding Today's Youth Culture* (Wheaton, IL: Tyndale House Publishers, 1999).
3. The videos *True Lies* and *Music to Die For* (both by Phil Chalmers) can be ordered at http://www.philchalmers.com. (The excellent resource *True Lies Street Drug Identification Guide* is also available through this website.)
4. *Plugged In* magazine is published monthly by Focus on the Family. Visit http://www.family.org/pplace/pi/ for more information.
5. The videos *Keys to Loving Relationships* and *Secrets to Lasting Love* are available through Smalley Relationship Center at http://smalley.gospelcom.net.

FAMILY SURVEYS—TOOLS FOR DISCOVERY

THE *FAMILY NEEDS SURVEY*

Led by Dennis Rainey, FamilyLife is one of the leading organizations in the world dedicated to helping families succeed. One of our favorite family resources for the church is FamilyLife's *Family Needs Survey*, a diagnostic tool designed to help individual churches look at the needs of their congregation with an emphasis on family and marriage issues. We know of several congregations who have been transformed by the survey. Just looking over the 31 common issues of the family will help you with your content focus as you partner with parents. (Note: Many thanks to FamilyLife for allowing us to adapt information from the *Family Needs Survey* material.)

DID YOU KNOW?

In the average church's adult congregation:

- 22 percent have been divorced
- 17 percent are in blended families
- 81 percent have been Christians over 10 years
- 75 percent say their most important need is spiritual growth

- 42 percent believe they have a good marriage
- 15 percent of married couples regularly pray together other than at mealtimes

As these startling statistics show, the average church comprises people with many different needs, and we need look no further than Jesus to know what we need to do. Jesus ministered to people's needs; when He met the Samaritan woman at the well (see John 4:1-26), He dealt with her inner thirst—something He continually did throughout His ministry.

The *Family Needs Survey* can help ministry leaders discover and prioritize the felt needs of families in their ministry so that they may lay a foundation for intentional ministry. It will also enable leaders to allocate scarce resources better and launch new programs with objective rationale. Covering a variety of topics like the congregation's demographics, marriage issues, general family issues, parenting issues, as well as spiritual activity, the results from the *Family Needs Survey* help church leaders to

- Be purposeful and intentional in ministering to families
- Discover and prioritize congregation needs objectively
- Provide valuable season of life information to teachers
- Build a family ministry that is focused, planned and confident

HOW THE SURVEY WORKS

The *Family Needs Survey* is a 49-question scannable form that would typically be distributed to adults in a congregation at the end of a Sunday service. The survey takes approximately 15 minutes to complete, and the completed surveys are returned to FamilyLife for analysis. The data in the survey is compiled into a report of over 100 pages, including charts and detailed explanations, and the report is sent to the participating church. FamilyLife will then follow up with the church through telephone calls to discuss the report findings.

ISSUES IDENTIFIED BY THE SURVEY

Thirty-one needs have been identified as the most common issues of families today. The *Family Needs Survey* questions help church leaders discover felt needs in their congregations in the areas of marriage, family and parenting. The following information explains each of the issues as defined in the survey:

General Issues

Establishing Adult Friendships
- Desire to experience more connection with other people
- Includes aspects of accountability, encouragement, transparency, support and having fun

Managing Finances/Money
- Desire to learn better spending and saving habits
- Includes aspects of debt, savings, budgeting, tithing, planning and associated attitudes

Growing in Relationship with God
- Desire for spiritual growth
- Includes theoretical and practical education; opportunities to experience worship, evangelism, fellowship, service and devotion

Managing Time
- Desire to learn planning skills to experience a less stressful life
- Includes tools (e.g., planners and PDAs) and planning margins for unexpected events

Selecting Wholesome Entertainment
- Desire to navigate family exposure to media
- Includes setting standards for movies, TV, radio, printed materials, music, etc.; then finding entertainment that fits set standards

Having Ministry in the Lives of Other People
- Desire to help others
- Includes using spiritual gifts, simple acts of love during

times of need and equipping others for better physical, mental, spiritual and emotional health

Handling Divorce
- Desire to heal after divorce
- Includes participation in large-group programs or one-on-one counseling and encouragement

Adjusting to Season of Life
- Desire to navigate aging process and its unique challenges
- Includes needs that are easily met and those that can require assistance

Adjusting to a Change in Employment
- Desire to address the stress of changing jobs
- Includes physical, emotional and other such responses

Developing and Maintaining Spiritual Disciplines
- Desire to practice spiritual activities on a regular basis
- Includes any activity that will help a relationship with God continue to grow

Dealing with Current or Past Drug and/or Alcohol Abuse
- Desire to be freed from addictive behavior and its results
- Includes involvement in large-group programs or one-on one counseling and encouragement

Dealing with Current or Past Sexual, Physical and/or Emotional Abuse
- Desire to heal from wounds of abusive experiences
- Includes learning new ways of thinking and breaking old patterns and habits

Developing Healthy Living and Eating Habits
- Desire to address physical condition
- Includes smoking and weight issues, sleeping habits and stress management

Marriage

Dating and Preparing for Marriage
• Desire to prepare for a godly marriage
• Includes learning about emotional, physical and mental attractions, dealing with baggage and helping potential mate to prepare for godly marriage

Understanding Different Personality Types
• Desire to understand characteristics of a mate
• Includes making wise adjustments in a relationship to help a mate reach his or her potential

Understanding Biblical Roles and Responsibilities in Marriage
• Desire to clear the blurred lines of marriage roles created by our culture
• Includes addressing men and women from a biblical perspective and redefining true headship and submission based on God's Word

Understanding Spouse's Needs and Expectations
• Desire to understand mate's perception of life
• Includes needs and expectations resulting from previous experiences instead of one's core characteristics

Developing and Maintaining Good Communication
• Desire to become transparent to one's mate
• Includes aspects of time management, learning new speaking or writing skills, dealing with past hurts and learning to become vulnerable

Developing and Maintaining Sexual Intimacy in Marriage
• Desire to understand sexual intimacy needs and God-given desires
• Includes issues of frequency, time, impotency, romance, pornography, adultery, abuse, etc., and learning how to have

a healthy, pure and exciting sexual relationship within marriage

Rekindling and Maintaining Romance
- Desire to improve emotional connection with one's mate
- Includes the areas of communication, respect, simple enjoyment of one another, spending time together, encouragement, complimenting and learning to improve in these areas

Building a Strong Marriage
- Desire to create an unbreakable marriage bond
- Includes learning how to be a good spouse, challenge one's spouse to grow, stay committed through the storms of life, be accountable and enjoy the ride called Life

Relating to In-Laws
- Desire to build a connection to mate's family
- Includes learning history, setting limits, learning new traditions and developing a willingness to change

Living in an Interfaith Marriage
- Desire to keep a marriage strong in spite of differences in religious beliefs between spouses
- Includes learning to depend on similarities instead of differences and how to negotiate for a win-win ending

Parenting

Developing and Sharpening Parenting Skills
- Desire to learn skills for becoming a better parent
- Includes recognizing parenting deficiencies and how to change them

Releasing and Moving a Child Toward Adult Independence
- Desire to learn how to let go as children grow up

- Includes preparing children for their adulthood and addressing one's own empty-nest emotions

Developing and Improving Family Communication
- Desire to increase transparency within one's family
- Includes creative time management, developing or improving speaking and writing skills, learning to accommodate others and creating an environment of emotional stability and security in the home

Developing a Child's Character, Identity and Morality
- Desire to learn skills for raising children to maturity
- Includes establishing what one's own beliefs are, and learning about the personality of a child and how best to teach the child so that he or she will reach his or her greatest potential

Disciplining a Child
- Desire to develop proper discipline for the benefit of the child
- Includes changing behavior through rewards and punishments, and creative ways to shape a child's behavior

Helping a Child Succeed at School
- Desire to give a child the best possible chance for success in school
- Includes practical education (the three Rs) and getting along with peers

Helping a Child Grow Spiritually
- Desire to increase a child's desire to know God
- Includes developing a home environment that promotes spiritual growth and providing opportunities and encouragement for spiritual growth outside the home

Establishing and Teaching Christian Values in the Home
- Desire to establish strong Christian values in a child

- Includes establishing what one's own values are and preparing oneself to pass on those values to a child intentionally

---

Contact FamilyLife at www.FamilyLife.com or 1-800-404-5052 extension 2554 to order a free copy of the *Family Needs Survey Information Package* for your church or ministry.

THE *ALL-CHURCH FAMILY SURVEY* AND THE *HEALTHY FAMILY SURVEY*

On pages 122-127 we've provided two excellent reproducible surveys based on the information in Jim's book *The Ten Building Blocks for a Happy Family*.[1] You'll find these surveys helpful for getting parents in your church to evaluate their own family's health and happiness. Because these surveys produce discussion and often help parents recognize needs, you may want to follow up by offering a class from Jim's book (yes, that's a plug—but it's a worthy one!), which offers excellent discussion starters at the end of each chapter. Many churches are also using Jim's video curriculum *Parenting Teens with Positive Results* as a way for parents to meet in a small group and discuss important topics covered in the survey.[2]

Notes
1. Jim Burns, *The Ten Building Blocks for a Happy Family* (Ventura, CA: Regal Books, 2003).
2. For more information or to order this video curriculum, visit www.youthbuilders.com.

ALL-CHURCH FAMILY SURVEY

1. What are your family's greatest needs?

2. What can our church do in the following areas to help families succeed?

   Children's ministry:

   Youth ministry:

   Parenting classes:

   Single parenting:

   Sermons:

   Other ideas:

3. If you were invited to attend and participate in periodic parenting seminars or workshops, would you attend?
   ❏ Yes   ❏ No

   If yes, what topics would be most beneficial for you and your family?

4. If our church had a parenting group that met regularly to go through practical, biblical material on parenting, would you be interested in participating?
   ❏ Yes   ❏ No

5. How can our church do a better job of helping families succeed?

6. Would you like guidance in mentoring and discipling your children to grow in their Christian faith?
   ❏ Yes   ❏ No

About You

Your name _____

Address _____

E-mail _____   Phone _____

About Your Children

Name   Age

_____   _____

_____   _____

_____   _____

_____   _____

_____   _____

_____   _____

HEALTHY FAMILY SURVEY

Here is a chance for you to measure the health and happiness of your family. Read through each one the following principles from the book *The Ten Building Blocks for a Happy Family* before you take the survey.[1] Then use a scale of 1 to 5 to rate how well you believe your family is doing with each principle (with 1 meaning We need a lot of improvement in this area and 5 meaning We're doing pretty good here). When finished, add up your score and decide what you can do to improve the health and happiness of your family!

TEN PRINCIPLES OF FAMILIES THAT SUCCEED

1. The Power of Being There　　　　_____

Children regard your very presence as a sign of caring and connectedness.

2. Express Affection, Warmth and Encouragement　_____

A family with a sense of affection, warmth and encouragement (as opposed to shame-based parenting) is a home where children and spouses feel more secure.

3. Build Healthy Morals and Values _____

The decisions kids make today will often affect them for the rest of their lives.

4. Discipline with Consistency _____

Clearly expressed expectations and consistent follow-through produce responsible kids.

5. Ruthlessly Eliminate Stress _____

The unbalanced life will not be kind to the areas we neglect.

6. Communication Is Key _____

Positive communication is the language of love for our children.

7. Play Is a Necessary Ingredient for a Close-Knit Family _____

There is nothing like play to bring about family togetherness and communication.

8. Love Your Spouse _____

A loving marriage brings hope and security to children.

9. The Best Things in Life Are Not Things _____

Healthy stewardship and financial decisions produce positive family priorities.

10. Energize Your Family's Spiritual Growth _____

Your greatest calling in life is to leave a spiritual legacy for your children.

TOTAL SCORE _____

SCORING

- **50 points.** Hello! Wake up! No family can be *that* healthy or that happy this side of heaven!
- **40 to 49 points.** Wow! You are definitely making some positive choices and important decisions about the health and happiness of your family. Your family will reap the benefits now and in the future.
- **30 to 39 points.** You're doing well. Which areas still need a bit of tweaking? Which action steps can you take to work toward greater family health?
- **20 to 29 points.** There is room for improvement. Where can you go for help? What decisions do you need to make to start improving your family life?
- **0 to 19 points.** Get help now! "Plans fail for lack of counsel, but with many advisers they succeed" (Proverbs 15:22). If you don't choose to get help and work on these important principles, your family's health and your children's future happiness will be in jeopardy.

Note
1. Jim Burns, *The Ten Building Blocks for a Happy Family* (Ventura, CA; Regal Books, 2003).

40 DAYS FOR THE FAMILY—AN OPPORTUNITY TO CONNECT

In 1999, inspired by a vision to help sustain and strengthen families within their communities, five men committed themselves and their resources to building strong families based on God's timeless principles. These men believed that the solid virtues produced and preserved in families—including the God-established concept of lifelong marriage between a man and a woman—were worthy of acknowledgment and celebration. From this desire to honor strong and healthy families, 40 Days for the Family was birthed.

Tim Smith was one of those five courageous men, and he is one of my (Jim's) heroes in the world of family ministry. While a youth worker, Tim was dedicated to family ministry, and as a writer and seminar speaker, his focus has continued to be on helping families succeed. Today, Tim is one of the key family pastors to the Church at large. His Life Skills for American Families ministry is one of the most comprehensive and finest family-ministry programs in existence today. I have been privileged to speak at his church on a regular basis and have seen firsthand the powerful effect of 40 Days for the Family. Tim was kind enough to allow us to pass on much of his information on this ministry to you. We have edited and adapted it, but the bulk of the material is from him.

EMPOWERING FAMILIES

The mission statement for 40 Days for the Family is simple and powerful. It reads "To celebrate and empower families with hope and inspiration through timeless principles and family-friendly opportunities that will lead to healthier, more vibrant communities."

40 Days for the Family is an annual 40-day program designed to remind communities about the importance of family life through events and activities that foster positive relationships among family members. During a 40-day period, families in the participating community are invited to participate in events throughout the community that will be fun, uplifting and educational.

Although the concepts of 40 Days for the Family are from Scripture and the historical example of Jesus Christ, individuals are not excluded from participation based on faith; this is a program which exists to strengthen communities. Those who have developed the program also acknowledge that a large majority of families do not fit the traditional model of a husband and wife with biological children. While the traditional model for family is the ideal, the program also works within the very real world of single-parent families, stepparent families, children raised by grandparents or foster families and families with adopted children. Each of these kinds of families needs to be affirmed, celebrated and empowered through discovering principles that will help them relate to each other and grow to be healthy families.

WORKING TOGETHER

Participating in a 40 Days for the Family program is a community effort. Primarily, there are three councils who work together to make the program a success in the community.

One—Church Council

A church council is a group of like-minded churches that values families and timeless principles. The goal is for the churches in the community to unite behind programs and emphasize building healthy families. Key leaders from each participating congregation work together to share resources and programming.

Two—Nonprofit Council

A nonprofit council is a group of nonprofit organizations who are whole-heartedly committed to strengthening and guiding a community by actively supporting families and activities that celebrate and empower—consistent with 40 Days for the Family's stated mission and objectives. This is the same concept as the church council, but it encourages various not-for-profit organizations (who already exist in your community) to come together and share resources, ideas and programs and to build a solid unifying role for the community.

Three—Business Council

A business council is a group of business leaders who believe in the mission of 40 Days for the Family and building healthy families in a vibrant community. These businesses can help with marketing and promoting the events, and possibly funding. Some businesses have donated food and other resources as well as loaned personnel to help give back to the community part of the investment the community has made in the business.

SHARED VALUES

The following value statements were put together by Life Skills for the American Family for its 40 Days for the Family ministry. Feel free to adapt these values to make this work for your church, organization or community.

What We Stand For

- Strong families as building blocks for a strong community
- Marriage between a man and a woman for life
- Effective parenting that considers each child's uniqueness
- Celebrating what is good, healthy and noble with today's family
- Empowering family members to relate in healthy ways
- Developing the whole individual—physically, socially, mentally, emotionally and spiritually
- Family-friendly awareness in our companies, businesses, government and community organizations

What We Value

- Celebrating and empowering families to enjoy greater fulfill-ment and spiritual growth through events and activities that inspire a fun and educational environment
- Timeless principles, such as mutual love and understanding, honesty, integrity, respect, faithfulness and selflessness
- Opportunities to celebrate and strengthen the family at home and in our community for 40 days of every year

How Your Faith-Based Organization Will Benefit

- Being involved helps promote you as family friendly and community minded.
- You are positioned with other like-minded organizations.
- You get exposed to a broader perspective and a different group than usual.
- You gain practical skills that families can build in the home on a daily or weekly basis.
- It's an opportunity for your organization and board to con-nect with the community in a new and different way.
- It helps you develop new services that meet the needs of families in your community.
- We can learn from each other how to address the issues of families and individuals in our community.
- It's a nonthreatening partnership.
- Stronger families build a stronger church (or faith-based organization).

CHALLENGING FAMILIES

The goal of the 40 Days for the Family program is to help families focus on an area of growth in order to learn new healthy-family practices that will continue the rest of the year.

THREE TRACKS TO CHOOSE FROM

There are three track options; each family chooses and focuses on one of the tracks based upon that family's area of needed growth. Within its chosen track, each family is challenged to choose from the exercises within that track—one daily, one weekly and one at any time during the 40 Days. Following is an explanation of each track, as well as a list of activities to choose from. (The intent of the exercises is that they also be continued throughout the rest of the year, continually strengthening the family unit.)

The Family Faith Challenge

This track focuses on deepening and strengthening the faith of a family. Here are the activities from which a family can choose. (Note: You could also adapt many of the "Fifty-Two Family Devotional Ideas" from this book's chapter 9 to fit this track.)

- Maintain a family prayer journal for 40 days.
- Attend a family worship concert.
- Have four family nights during the 40 days.
- Attend a family-night workshop to learn how to "do" family nights.
- Practice morning devotions as a family for 30 of the 40 days.

The Family Traditions Challenge

This track's goal is to establish consistent family traditions that will strengthen a family's identity. Here are the activities from which to choose for this track:

- Read a book as a family one night each week.
- Enjoy one meal as a family each day.
- Engage in creative discussions at that meal.
- Attend a father-son or mother-daughter event.
- Establish one of the new traditions found at the 40 Days website, www.40days.org.

The Community Connection Challenge

What better way is there to connect a family with its community than through service and expressions of gratitude? Here are the activities from which to choose for this track:

- Host a block party barbecue or picnic.
- Help with an existing community service project (hosted by a church or nonprofit organization).
- Visit three local sites in the community that may be new to you.
- Get involved in a "Make a Difference" note-writing project (developing gratitude).
- Choose from other family service project ideas found at the 40 Days website, www.40days.org.

SAMPLE FAMILY ACTIVITIES

The following is just a sample of ideas from the 40 Days ministry. As always, people support what they create (haven't we said that before?). We suggest you bring a family-ministry committee together—almost a full year in advance—to brainstorm, investigate and delegate great ideas for your specific situation.

CELEBRATE

- Father-Daughter Dance
- Family Western Dinner Dance
- Family Hike
- Family Cosmic Bowling
- Family Skate Day
- Family Fun Festival
- Family Worship Concert
- Family Dine Out
- Family Campout
- Family Beach Day
- Family Picnic and Chili Cookout
- Block Party Movie Night
- Family Boat Cruise
- Family Mountain-Bike Adventure
- High-Ropes Adventure Course
- Concerts in the Park
- Family Car Rally
- Family In-Line Skating

- Family Comedy Night
- Family Video/Film Festival
- Awards Night: Best in Family Media

EMPOWER

- Ten Great Dates
- Family Library Outing
- Family Museum Trip
- Family Letter-Writing Activity: "You Make a Difference"
- Family Life Arts Festival
- American Heritage Seminar
- Father-Kid Play Day
- Education Training Activity
- Family Food Drive (service project)
- Family Litter Pickup (parks and trails)
- Neighborhood Garage Sale (fund-raiser for charity)

- Clean the Closets for Charity (Salvation Army, etc.)
- Family Issues/Concerns Panel
- Family Forum: "Dealing with the Pace of Our Culture" (speaker series)
- Preparing for Kids (class)
- Empty-Nest Issues (speaker)
- Parenting Seminars[1]
- Fly Fishing and Life Workshop
- Safety Workshop (parents and kids together)
- Family Free-Meals Program (service project)

HOW YOUR ORGANIZATION CAN GET INVOLVED

There are many ways to get involved in 40 Days for the Family, and many levels of involvement. You can contact 40 Days for the Family at www.40days.org. Meantime, here are a few ideas that have worked for other organizations who saw the value of strengthening families through this program:

- If you have an existing program or service that fits the basic concept of 40 Days for the Family, adapt it to the 40-Days format for more exposure and participation.
- Create a new program or service that will meet needs not currently being met.

- Tie in with and support 40 Days programs already existing in your area that are in line with your mission and values. (No programming on your part!)
- Work with other 40 Days faith-based groups to develop a collaborative project.

FAQs

As we mentioned, Tim Smith is one of the key experts in the world on family ministry. Here are several questions and answers to give you a quick overview of what 40 Days for the Family is about so that you can share the information easily with your ministry leaders:

- **What is 40 Days for the Family?** It is a grassroots, volunteer effort designed to strengthen the community by strengthening the family through an annual concentrated 40-day emphasis designed to provide community members with visible reminders of the importance of family life.

- **What goes on during the program?** Events and activities that foster positive relationships among family members occur throughout the 40-day experience.

- **Who is behind 40 Days for the Family?** Life Skills for the American Family, a nondenominational, public-benefit 501(c)(3), nonprofit organization.

- **Do we really need 40 days to celebrate the family?** No. We should support the family 365 days a year because that's how often our families are under attack. However, by setting aside an intense period of activity—and through involvement, education, promotion and editorial coverage—we can emphasize the positive relationship between strong and healthy families and strong and healthy communities.

- **How has 40 Days for the Family supported the family in the past?** The first event of this kind happened in 2002 in the greater Conejo Valley in Southern California. This first year, more than 16,000 people participated in 62 events that were coordinated, hosted and/or supported by 20 local churches, 12 nonprofit organizations and 10 large local businesses. The committees generated impressive funding to make it a very visible event and created significant awareness in the Conejo Valley. Since the very conception of the program, 40 Days for the Family has been about strengthening, encouraging and empowering families.

- **Why are faith-based organizations invited to participate in this effort?** First, the Judeo-Christian faith tradition—so clearly fundamental in the history of the United States—is the single most important foundation supporting and protecting our American communities. The healthy family sustained by this faith foundation embraces love, compassion, patience, kindness and self-control. These qualities are rooted in our faith. Above all, we believe that a dedicated faith in God offers the strongest support system that a family can embrace. In short, God is the only enduring nucleus that keeps families intact, content and focused on a future of hope and promise.

  Second, any successful grassroots effort must be interwoven with the institutions that make our communities work. Faith-based institutions provide support for families 365 days a year. An intense focus on celebrating and empowering families in our communities cannot be successful without effectively partnering with the faith community to help promote and operate a portion of the initial 40-day window. The objective is to expose families who otherwise would not visit your house of worship to events at your location designed to strengthen and empower families.

- **Will all of the activities in this event be religious?** No. However, even though they are not designed to be vehicles for proselytizing, they will be faith-friendly and not hostile or adversarial to traditional Judeo-Christian beliefs.

- **Are the activities open to the public?** Yes! Even though a seminar or event may be hosted at a church, people from outside that particular church are welcome to attend.

- **Is 40 Days for the Family affiliated with or supported by any one religion or church?** No. On a personal level, each member of the board of directors is deeply committed to serving God, active in church life and committed personally to representing Him to their own families and community.

- **What qualities were the founders of 40 Days for the Family looking for in potential faith participants when 40 Days first began?** Participants needed a passion to reach out into the community to meet the needs of all families. 40 Days envisions participation by faith-based participants who are willing to partner with other institutions for the good of families in the community. Participants should want to help celebrate, empower and embrace the value families bring to children, adults, community and society as a whole.

- **What qualities should lay leaders have?** Lay leaders need to have passion for the family unit. They should also be people who can make things happen, who are encouraged by large-scale coordinated challenges and who are not intimidated by being highly visible to community and media. These leaders need to possess a passion to work with like-minded people of faith in an effort to return the family to a place of respect. They should strongly believe that families are a God-established unit, the very building blocks of love and compassion that help build happy, healthy lives and a secure society. Last but not least, they should be willing to make a stand for the values espoused by 40 Days for the Family.

Note
1. Visit www.youthbuilders.com for more information about Traits of a Healthy Family Parenting Seminars.

RESOURCES

The world of family-based youth ministry and family ministry in general is growing at a very rapid pace. Because of the amount of interest and questions we receive, we are offering a list of our favorite books and resources. We do this at the risk of neglecting to include many great resources, some of which were written after the publication of this book. We are deeply grateful to Dave Chow, youth pastor at the Crystal Cathedral, YouthBuilders trainer, family-ministry expert and our good friend, for his help and expertise in compiling this list of resources.

GENERAL FAMILY MINISTRY

Ambrose, Dub, and Walt Mueller. *Ministry to Families with Teenagers.* Loveland, CO: Group Books, 1988.
   This book provides a good overview of how and why to minister to families with teenagers. While it provides a solid foundation for effective family ministry, it is also full of practical suggestions. The book is divided into four sections: "Why Minister to Families with Teenagers?" "Elements of a Successful Ministry," "Building a Ministry to Families with Teenagers" and "Programming Ideas."

Clapp, Rodney. *Families at the Crossroads.* Downers Grove, IL: InterVarsity Press, 1993.
   After addressing the historical, biblical and cultural views of the family, Clapp argues for a proper biblical understanding of the family in the context of our society—especially in the Church. He argues strongly that the family of God (the Church) should exert more

influence than the individual family and that our culture tends to overemphasize the individual family, to the detriment of the family of God.

Clark, Chap. *The Youth Worker's Handbook for Family Ministry*. Grand Rapids, MI: Zondervan Publishing House, 1997.

This book highlights the different perspectives of family ministry. You'll learn the right questions to ask when developing a ministry to families, and you'll find helpful ideas and strategies for getting your family ministry up and running. The book is divided into five sections: "Defining Family Ministry," "Creating a Successful Family Ministry," "Involving Moms and Dads in Family Ministry," "Programming Your Family Ministry" and "Providing Materials to Strengthen Families Where They Live."

DeVries, Mark. *Family-Based Youth Ministry*. Downers Grove, IL: InterVarsity Press, 1994.

A must-read for anyone considering doing family ministry. This was the first book to offer a paradigm shift for youth ministry in the 1990s. Much of the book focuses on analyzing the problems in today's youth culture and the overall ineffectiveness of current youth-ministry models. Family-based ministry calls for a radical shift from the current youth-centered model to a family-based model where adult-to-student encounters and activities form the foundation of the youth ministry. Several suggestions are made throughout the book for implementing a family-based youth ministry, but the general tone is theoretical and sociological.

Erwin, Pamela. *The Family-Powered Church*. Loveland, CO: Group Publishing, 2000.

This book takes a look at family ministry from the perspective of the Church as a loving and committed community of faith. Erwin encourages the Church to help families pass on their stories, develop rituals and develop rites of passage, and she shares ideas on connecting members within a family, connecting families to other families and connecting generations.

Freudenberg, Ben, and Rick Lawrence. *The Family-Friendly Church*. Loveland, CO: Vital Ministry, 1998.

An excellent book that discusses the need for churches to transition from a church-centered, home-supported ministry to a home-centered, church-supported ministry. After helping the reader understand the significant difference between the two, the authors offer several examples and ideas in how to move one's church toward the latter model. Special emphasis is put on how best to connect the home and church. Highly recommended.

Garland, Diana. *Family Ministry: A Comprehensive Guide*. Downers Grove, IL: InterVarsity Press, 1999.

This is the most comprehensive book to date on the topic of family ministry. The book is divided into six major sections: "The Context for Family Ministry," "The Processes of Family Life," "The History of Families and the Church," "Biblical Foundations for Family Ministry Today," "Planning and Leading Family Ministry" and "Ministry with Specific Family Relationships." While enormous in size (more than 600 pages), it is a worthwhile read for anyone serious about doing family ministry.

Guernsey, Dennis. *A New Design for Family Ministry*. Elgin, IL: David C. Cook, 1982.

Based on the belief that family is the most significant socializing agent for an individual, the author outlines the Church's role as empowering, networking and equipping families to be effective socializing institutions. Drawing from the insights of "systems theory," the author shares ideas and strategies on how a church and its pastor can accomplish the task of ministering to families.

Hebbard, Don. *The Complete Handbook for Family-Life Ministry in the Church*. Nashville, TN: Thomas Nelson, 1995.

Hebbard begins by addressing the importance of family ministry and the common barriers it faces, and then lays out a strategy for family ministry that includes assessing congregational needs, programming for felt needs, effective outreach to unchurched families, the role and place for counseling, the different models of family ministry and the necessary skills for a family minister.

Justice, Mike. *It Takes a Family to Raise a Youth Ministry*. Kansas City, MO: Beacon Hill Press, 1998.

In this very short (but definitely worthwhile) book, the author argues for the need of youth ministries to shift from a youth-only focus to a ministry-to-families-with-teens focus. After presenting different models for family ministry and obstacles to watch for, the author lays out a strategy for implementing family ministry.

Lyon, Brynoll K., and Archie Smith, eds. *Tending the Flock: Congregations and Family Ministry*. Louisville, KY: Westminster John Knox Press, 1998.

This book is a unique contribution to the world of family ministry. Each chapter shares how different churches are addressing the family issues they face. The churches examined are diverse in their denominations, church sizes and specific issues.

Money, Royce. *Ministering to Families: A Positive Plan of Action*. Abilene, TX: ACU Press, 1987.

An early contribution to the field of family ministry addressing the why, what and how of family ministry. While relatively basic in content, this book can help in laying a good foundation for starting a family ministry.

Sell, Charles. *Family Ministry*. Grand Rapids, MI: Zondervan Publishing House, 1995.

This book is a fairly comprehensive presentation on family ministry and reads like a textbook—but it provides a solid theological basis for the issues involved in family ministry. Practical applications of these theological principles are offered with the insights of other disciplines such as sociology, psychology and other social sciences.

Strommen, Merton, and Richard Hardel. *Passing On the Faith*. Winona, MN: Saint Mary's Press/Christian Brothers Publications, 2000.

The authors of this book share extensive experience in youth and family ministry research. Numerous examples and strategies to develop strong youth and families are provided.

Thomas, Steve. *Your Church Can Be—Family Friendly*. Joplin, MO: College Press Publishing Company, 1997.

This book describes in detail the author's personal journey from youth ministry to family ministry. In a very personal way, Thomas helps the reader to understand his passion for family ministry and the changes that needed to take place in his church.

Wallace, Eric. *Uniting the Church and Home: Solutions for Integrating Church and Home*. Self-Published, 1999.

Recognizing the discontinuity in terms of faith formation and focus, Wallace seeks to find contact between the church and home, and help facilitate renewal and rebuilding between them. This nine-page booklet is self-published and may be difficult to obtain in bookstores.

Waugh, Phillip. *Leading Family Ministry in a Church*. Nashville, TN: LifeWay Press, 1998.

Another very short but worthwhile book, this resource focuses on assessing, designing and implementing a family ministry and contains many helpful charts and diagrams.

PROGRAMMING TOOLS FOR FAMILY MINISTRY

130 Ways to Involve Parents in Youth Ministry. Loveland, CO: Group Publishing, 1994.

As the title implies, this book is a compilation of 130 ideas from various individuals on how to involve parents in youth ministry. Some ideas are relatively thorough and detailed while others are more brief.

Buller, Bob, ed. *Family-Friendly Ideas Your Church Can Do*. Loveland, CO: Group Publishing, 1998.

A highly practical book with more than 50 ideas that families can do in the following categories: learning activities, worship experiences, service projects, enrichment activities and fun times.

Fun Ideas for the Family-Friendly Church. Loveland, CO: Group Publishing, 2000.

This book includes 50 fun and practical ideas for learning, worshiping, serving and building relationships.

Habermas, Ron, and Davis Olshine. *Tag-Team Youth Ministry*. Cincinnati, OH: Standard Publishing, 1995.

A short book that briefly discusses the philosophy behind family ministry. Includes 50 practical ideas on how to move your ministry towards a family-based model.

Lytle, Tom; Kelly Schwartz; and Gary Hartke. *101 Ways to be Family Friendly in Youth Ministry*. Kansas City, MO: Beacon Hill Press, 1996.

This book has more than 100 ideas to make your youth ministry family friendly.

Nappa, Mike and Amy. *Imagine That! 365 Wacky Ways to Build a Creative Christian Family*. Minneapolis, MN: Augsburg, 1998.

This book highlights more than 300 ways families can build creativity and unity in their homes.

Simpson, Amy, ed. *No More Us and Them*. Loveland, CO: Group
    Publishing, 1999.
    A practical book sharing 100 different ways to bring youth and church
    together.

PARENTING AND FAMILY BOOKS BY JIM BURNS

Burns, Jim. *The Ten Building Blocks for a Happy Family*. Ventura, CA:
    Regal Books, 2003.
Burns, Jim, and Steve Arterburn. *Drugproof Your Kids*. Ventura, CA:
    Regal Books, 1995.
————. *Parents' Guide to Top Ten Dangers Teens Face*. Wheaton, IL:
    Tyndale House Publishers, 1999.

PARENTING AND FAMILY BOOKS
BY VARIOUS AUTHORS

Chapman, Gary. *The Five Love Languages*. Chicago, IL: Northfield
    Publishing, 1992.
————. *The Five Languages of Love of Teenagers*. Chicago, IL: Northfield
    Publishing, 2000.
Chapman, Gary, and Ross Campbell. *The Five Love Languages of
    Children*. Chicago, IL: Northfield Publishing, 1997.
Cline, Foster W., and Jim Fay. *Parenting with Love and Logic: Teaching
    Children Responsibility*. Colorado Springs, CO: NavPress, 1990.
Dobson, James. *The Strong-Willed Child*. Wheaton, IL: Tyndale House, 1992.
Elkind, David. *All Grown Up and No Place to Go: Teenagers in Crisis*.
    Reading, MA: Perseus Publishing, 1997.
Glenn, H. Stephen, and Jane Nelsen. *Raising Self-Reliant Children in a
    Self-Indulgent World*. Roseville, CA: Prima Publishing, 2000.
Huggins, Kevin. *Parenting Adolescents*. Colorado Spring, CO: Navpress,
    1992.
Leman, Kevin. *Making Children Mind Without Losing Yours*. Grand
    Rapids, MI: Fleming H. Revell Company, 2000.
Mueller, Walt. *Understanding Today's Youth Culture*. Wheaton, IL:

Tyndale House Publishers, 1999.

Rainey, Dennis and Barbara, and Bruce Nygren. *Parenting Today's Adolescent*. Nashville, TN: Thomas Nelson, 1998.

Smalley, Gary. *The Key to Your Child's Heart*. Dallas, TX: Word Publishing, 1995.

———. *Making Love Last Forever*. Dallas, TX: Word Publishing, 1997.

Smalley, Gary and John Trent. *The Blessing*. Nashville, TN: Thomas Nelson, 1990.

Trent, John. *Be There! Making Connections in a Disconnected World*. Colorado Springs, CO: WaterBrook Press, 2000.

———. *Parents' Guide to the Spiritual Mentoring of Teenagers*. Wheaton, IL: Tyndale House Publishers, 1995.

Weidmann, Jim, et al. *Spiritual Milestones: A Guide to Celebrating Your Child's Spiritual Passages*. Colorado Springs, CO: Chariot Victor Publishing, 2001.

VIDEO CURRICULUM

Burns, Jim. *Parenting Teenagers for Positive Results: An Interactive Video Course*. Loveland, CO: Group Publishing, 2001.

This kit could change everything for the teen-blessed families in your congregation! There is perhaps no better way to develop parenting skills than by comparing notes with youth culture and family expert Jim Burns (via video); watching humorous family vignettes featuring "real" family situations; and sharing with other parents of teens and preteens in an interactive, guided, small-group setting. Parents will be better equipped to parent their teens, encouraged and affirmed in their role, and be able to forge lifeline friendships with other parents, so they can navigate the teen years with strength and confidence. This curriculum includes a video, leader's guide and six participant guides.

———. *YouthBuilders Training to Go*. Ventura, CA: Gospel Light, 2000.

Sixteen-part video series for youth workers.

Burns, Jim, and Steve Arterburn. *Drugproof Your Kids Video*. Ventura, CA: Gospel Light, 1995.

Studies have shown that 85 percent of all young people say they have experimented with intoxicating substances—a statistic that includes children from strong Christian families. But there is something parents can do. This video features practical, biblical steps to head off or, if necessary, work through a drug crisis. Parents will come to understand why any child—*including theirs*—is at risk of abusing drugs and alcohol.

Huggins, Kevin. *Parenting Adolescents Video Curriculum*. Colorado Springs, CO: NavPress, 1992.

Based on *Parenting Adolescents* by Kevin Huggins, this video series seeks to encourage and equip parents to raise godly kids. The needs, conflicts, depth of character and spiritual maturity of parents are a large focus in this video series. This is a more in-depth examination of parenting than is *Understanding Your Teenager Video Curriculum*.

Rice, Wayne, and Ken Davis. *Understanding Your Teenager Video Curriculum*. El Cajon, CA: Youth Specialties, 1992.

This six-part video series deals with important issues and topics in understanding teenagers. The video segments are short and meant to promote discussion—a good resource to use for a parenting series or a potential outreach event to unchurched parents.

WEBSITES

40 Days for the Family
http://www.40days.org

Center for Parent/Youth Understanding
http://www.cpyu.org

Christian Education Counselor
http://www.cecounselor.ag.org

Family Life
http://www.familylife.com

Focus on the Family
http://www.family.org

Gary Smalley
http://www.garysmalley.com

Group's Youth Ministry Online
http://www.youthministry.com

Heritage Builders
http://www.heritagebuilders.com

Hispanic Ministry Center
http://www.hmconline.org

John Trent
http://www.strongfamilies.com

Josh McDowell Ministry
http://www.joshmcdowell.com

Movie Reviews
http://www.ScreenIt.com

National Network of Youth Ministries
http://www.youthworkers.net

***Plugged In* Magazine**
http://www.PluggedInMagazine.com

Purpose-Driven Youth Ministry
http://www.pdym.com

Reach-Out Youth Solutions
http://www.reach-out.org

Russ Cline, Youth World
http://www.youthworld.org.ec

Simply Youth Ministry
http://www.simplyyouthministry.com

Understanding Your Teenager
http://www.uyt.com

Young Life
http://www.younglife.org

Youth for Christ
http://www.yfc.org

Youth Specialties
http://www.youthspecialties.com

YouthBuilders
http://www.youthbuilders.com

GOD'S WORD FOR A JR. HIGH WORLD

"This is the best junior high/middle school curriculum to come out in years. Creativity and biblical integrity are evident on every page. Students will love it."
Jim Burns, Ph.D.
President
National Institute of Youth Ministry

Young people between the ages of 11 and 14 are the most open to who Jesus is and what a life with Him offers. Reach them with Pulse—designed especially for them!

Throughout the cutting-edge series, three categories of study help junior highers understand and apply God's Word in their lives: Biblical, Life Issues and Discipleship.

Connect with junior highers—get all the Pulse studies!

#1 Christianity: the Basics
ISBN 08307.24079

#2 Prayer
ISBN 08307.24087

#3 Friends
ISBN 08307.24192

#4 Teachings of Jesus
ISBN 08307.24095

#5 Followers of Christ
ISBN 08307.24117

#6 Teens of the Bible
ISBN 08307. 24125

#7 Life at School
ISBN 08307.25083

#8 Miracles of Jesus
ISBN 08307.25091

#9 Home and Family
ISBN 08307.25105

#10 Genesis
ISBN 08307.25113

#11 Fruit of the Spirit
ISBN 08307.25474

#12 Feelings & Emotions
ISBN 08307.25482

#13 Peer Pressure
ISBN 08307.25490

#14 Reaching Your World
ISBN 08307.25504

Available at your local Christian bookstore.
www.gospellight.com

Gospel Light

More from Jim Burns,
the Youth Ministry Expert!

Wake 'Em Up!

This fresh-roasted blend of sizzling hot resources helps you turn youth meetings into dynamic events that kids look forward to. Successfully field-tested in youth groups and edited by youth expert **Jim Burns**, **Fresh Ideas** will wake 'em up and get your group talking.

Illustrations, Stories and Quotes to Hang Your Message On
ISBN 08307.18834

Case Studies, Talk Sheets and Discussion Starters
ISBN 08307.18842

Games, Crowdbreakers & Community Builders
ISBN 08307.18818

Bible Study Outlines and Messages
ISBN 08307.18850

Skits & Dramas
ISBN 08307.18826

Missions and Service Projects
ISBN 08307.18796

Incredible Retreats
ISBN 08307.24036

Worship Experiences
ISBN 08307.24044

Instant Bible Studies
ISBN 08307.29194

Intense Illustrations
ISBN 08307.29208

Hot Topics
ISBN 08307.29216

Holidays and Special Events
ISBN 08307.29224

To wake up your youth, contact your local Christian bookstore. **www.gospellight.com**

Gospel Light

More Great Ways to Reach and Teach Young People

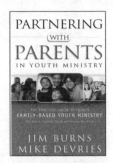

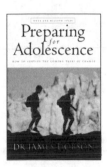
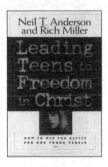